Simply Italian

Simply Italian

COOKING AT HOME WITH
THE CHIAPPA SISTERS

Michela, Emanuela
and Romina Chiappa

MICHAEL JOSEPH
an imprint of
PENGUIN BOOKS

MICHAEL JOSEPH

Published by the Penguin Group

Penguin Books Ltd, 80 Strand, London WC2R 0RL, England

Penguin Group (USA) Inc., 375 Hudson Street, New York, New York 10014, USA

Penguin Group (Canada), 90 Eglinton Avenue East, Suite 700, Toronto, Ontario, Canada M4P 2Y3
(a division of Pearson Penguin Canada Inc.)

Penguin Ireland, 25 St Stephen's Green, Dublin 2, Ireland (a division of Penguin Books Ltd)

Penguin Group (Australia), 250 Camberwell Road,
Camberwell, Victoria 3124, Australia (a division of Pearson Australia Group Pty Ltd)

Penguin Books India Pvt Ltd, 11 Community Centre,
Panchsheel Park, New Delhi – 110 017, India

Penguin Group (NZ), 67 Apollo Drive, Rosedale, Auckland 0632, New Zealand
(a division of Pearson New Zealand Ltd)

Penguin Books (South Africa) (Pty) Ltd, Block D, Rosebank Office Park,
181 Jan Smuts Avenue, Parktown North, Gauteng 2193, South Africa

Penguin Books Ltd, Registered Offices: 80 Strand, London WC2R 0RL, England

www.penguin.com

First published 2014
003

Text copyright © Michela, Emanuela and Romina Chiappa, 2013
Photography copyright © Mark Read, 2013,
with additional photography from Rahel Weiss and Leo Ferenc, 2013

Set in Archer and HT Pasticceria

Printed in China
Colour Reproduction by Alta Image Ltd

A CIP catalogue record for this book is available from the British Library

ISBN: 978-0-718-17705-8

FSC
www.fsc.org
MIX
Paper from
responsible sources
FSC™ C018179

Penguin Books is committed to a sustainable
future for our business, our readers and
our planet. This book is made from Forest
Stewardship Council™ certified paper.

Contents

Nonno's Poem

This is a nonsense poem our Nonno used to tell us as kids. It always made us giggle and we thought it would be a perfect introduction to our book, memories of fun family times in the Chiappa household.

Mezza notte in punto,
una giornata splendida.
Il sole cadeva a grande falde,
la neve con i suoi raggi possenti
riscaldava la terra.

It was precisely midnight,
A beautiful sunny day.
The sun was falling down in large flakes,
The snow with its powerful rays
Warming up the earth.

Io e te eravamo in tre.
Eravam seduti su un grosso
sassolino di legno al chiaror di
una candela spenta
leggevamo un libro senza parole.

You and me together made three.
We sat on a huge wooden pebble,
In the faint glimmer of a burnt-out candle
We read an unwritten novel.

Vedemmo un cadavere vivente,
che allontanandosi si avvicinava.
Io presi paura e salii su un fico
mangiando delle prugne.

We saw a living corpse,
Disappearing, it still edged closer.
Struck with fear I climbed a fig tree
Whilst eating some plums.

Il padron delle zucche
mi morse con un coltello
senza manico e mancante la pura lama.

The pumpkin farmer
Bit me with a knife
Missing its handle and its
razor-sharp blade.

E mi disse:
Muori ho scellerato che hai mangiato
lo zucchero salato!

And he said to me:
Die, you truthful liar,
Because you have eaten the salty sugar!

To our cooking mentors, teachers and inspiration:
our *nonne* and Mum

Introduction

Wales and Italy, family and food. For us, these four things are inextricably linked and at the root of our upbringing. Whether at our family home in Wales or on holiday in the small hilltop village in northern Italy where we are from, we have always heard Dad say that *la tavola* (the table) is the central focus of our lives – it's where we cook, eat and socialize.

The three of us – Michela, Emanuela and Romina – grew up living in what some might call an entourage, a brood or even a clan of family in the Welsh valleys near Merthyr Tydfil. Our first home was a set of terraced houses on the side of a hill overlooking Merthyr Tydfil, where Dad had grown up with his own aunts, uncles and cousins. We later moved into one long farmhouse with interconnecting doors, with views of Aberdare. We were in one house, where our Mum and Dad, Paola and Graziano, still live. Next door is our Uncle Laz (Dad's brother), his wife Giulia and their two daughters Antonella and Grazia, and next to them lived our Italian grandparents, Nonno Pino and Nonna Luisa.

Nonno Pino came from a tiny village called Pilati on the top of the Apennine Mountains in Emilia Romagna between Bardi, Bedonia and Borgo Val di Taro. He lived off the land through seasonal farming jobs such as lumber jacking, carpentry and goat or pig farming – basically, anything he could put his hands to!

Our Nonna came from a middle-class family. She would often tell us how Nonno hadn't wanted to marry her; he said he had nothing to give her and therefore she couldn't marry him. He would say, 'I'm a simple farmer and all I do is dig holes for potatoes.' Her loving response was, 'Well then, you can dig the hole and I'll be there to place the potato.' They soon married.

'WALES *and* ITALY, FAMILY *and* FOOD.
*For us, these four things are inextricably linked
and at the root of our upbringing.'*

After World War II ended, Italy was in the midst of a financial depression and many Italians emigrated abroad to find better opportunities. When Dad was three years old, Nonno and Nonna decided to follow many other Bardigiani to Wales, where there was already a thriving Italian community. Nonno was a plumber and, although he didn't speak a word of English, he managed to earn a decent living working for the Italian families and never had reason to learn the language!

Our grandparents, like most people at that time, had to live a simple life but even with the most basic ingredients Nonna always rustled up delicious, hearty Italian meals. *La cucina povera* (peasant food) can be a rich feast if you know how! She developed clever substitutes for ingredients that they couldn't afford – a block of Cheddar, for example, air-dried for several weeks until it is as hard as rock, can be used instead of Parmesan. Obviously the real thing is preferable but Nonna used to say that you have to make the best of what you can afford.

Our other grandparents, on Mum's side of the family, are the Ferrari-Lanes from Porthcawl in South Wales. Nonna Anna was originally from Bettola (a little Italian town about an hour from Bardi and Piacenza) whereas Nonno Muk-a-Muk, as we called him (real name Morwood), is our Welsh/English connection. He was a master baker and owned his own café and bakery in Bridgend – this is where we get all our baking secrets. Romina takes after him and has written down all of his recipes. Nonno's speciality was puff pastry and he made the BEST coffee puffs! He was also influenced by our Italian side – see Nonno's Mini Sausage Rolls on page 149.

The Italian immigrant community in Wales is now very well established – so much so that there is a society called the *Amici Val Ceno* (Friends of the Ceno, which is the river that runs through the Bardi valley). The society hosts events throughout the year, but the highlight of the calendar is the annual Italian Picnic – *La Scampagnata*. On one weekend in June, friends and family congregate in a field in Wales to eat together, but this isn't an average picnic with a few sandwiches and a blanket spread out on the grass; Italians take picnics very seriously! Everyone turns up in vans with gazebos, garden furniture and barbecues, unveiling container after container of freshly prepared food. The day is spent eating and visiting each other's tables to see who has cooked the best and the most that year.

Ricetta Elsa. VOV.

- 1 litro latte
- 8 uova solo il rosso
- 2 etti di zucchero a velo
- 2 etti marsala
- ? etti alcol fino
- 6 etti zucchero normale

Bollite il latte con lo zucchero leggermente per mezz'ora e lasciarlo raffreddare, sbattere le uova con lo zucchero a velo per ½ 30 minuti, unire il marsala con l'alcol rimestando bene, lasciarlo ... per qualche ora, prima d'imbottigliare.

Bagna «Lisa»

... senza d'aglio, tagliarla e fare in un bicchiere a mezzo di acqua ... le acciughe sotto sale su acqua
Pulirla ... Aggiungerle all'aglio + olio + burro ... cuocere bene suo un po' di ... aggiunge un po' di ...

Torta di mele

uova 3/4 di tazza di zucchero, mezza tazza di olio di mais, 3 cucchiai da tavola di acqua, 1 bustina di vaniglia, 1 pizzico di sale, 2 tazze e mezza di farina, 2 cucchiai da tavola di lievito Magic Baking oppure 1 bustina di lievito Bertolini, mezzo limone spremuto.
2 o 3 mele tagliate a fette
Lavorare uova e zucchero, aggiungere olio acqua farina, mettere circa metà pasta, poi le fettine di mele e coprire della pasta
Metterla nel forno già caldo per circa 40 minuti
Buon appetito un bacio

Ginepro

- ... branche di ginepro
- ... l. di alcool
- ... kg d'acqua

Dolce Freddo (Elsa).

Ingredienti:
6 uova, 12 cucchiai di zucchero a velo, 1 scatola di mascarpone da mezzo chilo (oppure panna??), 2 scatole di biscotti Pavesini.
Si lavorano i tuorli d'uova con lo zucchero, e le chiare a neve, si unisce il mascarpone, o panna, formando una crema, si bagnano i biscotti con caffè forte, o liquore a piacere, facendo uno strato di crema, uno di biscotti, si mette in frigo almeno un'ora prima di servirli.
Fate un liquore: caffè 3 etti (9 oz), ... zucchero, facendo bollire per qualche minuto in 135 grammi (4 oz) d'acqua, a parte fate un caffè forte con 70 grammi di caffè (2 oz) con 225 grammi (7 oz) ...

---

d'acqua. Unitela al sciroppo di zucchero, tenendo tutto ben coperto che non svapori, unendo anche una bustina di vaniglia ... e 12 grammi di alcol per liquore e zucchero quando tutto è freddo e poi imbottigliare.

Torta di zabaglione.
Fate una buona pasta frolla dividetela a metà e con una metà foderare una teglia già imburrata, stendervi uno strato di marmellata buona, poi fare un altro strato di savoiardi, quindi ricoprirli con uno strato di zabaglione ancora caldo e fatto con liquore forte. Ricoprite con l'altra pasta frolla e cuocere al forno.

Liquore di caffè

Far sciogliere 3 etti di zucchero in 125 di acqua calda.
Fare poi il caffè con ... Di caffè e 225 gr ... acqua unire alle ... sciolto
Do tutto e freddo gr 125 di alcol ... e una bustina ... iglia
... che le riuscirà
Affettuosi saluti
Fiorenza
...-8-1960

... 2 di zucchero
... 1 di cioccolato in ...
... di burro fresco. uova 4

Lavorazione
... mescolo molto bene il burro fresco finché è ben liscio, si mescolano i rossi d'uova, a parte si sbattono i bianchi alla neve in ... aggiungendo un cucchiaio di zucchero si mescola, si divide poi a metà in una metà ... il cioccolato, si mette un po' di liquore, si bagnano i biscotti in ... tutte due le parti, si schiacciano intorno alla forma ... liquore e si ricoprono all'interno ... fanno i strati diversi e si ricopron all'esterno ... i biscotti, mette la forma nel frigorifero.

Si fa sciogliere in 70 grammi di burro si fa ... un po' alla ... farina rimestando, ... ci si aggiunge ... fino alla fine ...

---

lievito vanigliato
PANE degli ANGELI

LIEVITO VANIGLIATO

RICETTAR...
PER CROSTA...
TORTE SALATE E PIZ...
DA PIC-N...

Bertolini

Panna cot...
1 litro Panna
200 grammi ...
5 foglie Co... (gel...

'All the recipes Nonna cooked have been passed through mum to us. This book is a collection of those recipes, as well as others deciphered from Nonna's notebooks.'

In much the same way, each summer the Welsh–Italians flock back to Bardi for some festivities – the highlight being the *Festa Dell' Emigrante*, held in the town centre, where you'll find a huge feast of local delicacies like cured meats, pasta with porcini and wild boar with polenta. The food is spread out on trestle tables and accompanied by lots of wine. There's dancing and even the *cuccagna* – a greased telephone pole that teams compete to shimmy up to win prizes. The funny thing is that the locals will often hear strong Welsh accents calling out across from one end of the bar to the other.

So, as you can see, we've been surrounded by family and food throughout our lives. As soon as we could walk we were helping out in the kitchen. Even though we were more likely to crack eggshell into the pasta dough, or get flour all over the floor, we always had a role in the kitchen. When you're young, it's the best time to learn about food. And all the recipes Nonna cooked have been passed through Mum to us. This book is a collection of those recipes, as well as others deciphered from Nonna's notebooks. And we've also included little tips and tricks that we hope you find useful. We don't claim to be professional chefs and we believe that cooking should be enjoyable – so just give it a go and play around with it!

Whilst our grandparents were able to spend lots of time in the kitchen, most people today need to fit cooking into their already busy lives, and home cooking often comes lower down in the list of priorities. With this book we want to show you how you can manage both; all three of us have hectic lives and careers but we also place huge importance on our traditions and family way of life.

A traditional Italian meal has more courses than a British menu (sometimes many more!). We usually start with an *antipasto*, followed by the *primo piatto* (which is usually a pasta dish), then the *secondo* (meat or fish) with a selection of *contorni* (sides), and finishing with *dolci (dessert)*. As well as recipes for the traditional meals we eat at Casa Chiappa, we've included a few that we only eat in Italy and also some Welsh-inspired recipes. After all, you can take the girl out of Wales . . . In our Channel 4 television series, *Simply Italian*, we focused on pasta, but here we share with you the whole range – from snacks, soups and salads to mains, side dishes, desserts and cakes. Good, simple, fresh Italian food, which fits into our modern lifestyles without any fuss.

About the Sisters

MICHELA (or Miki) travels the world with her job for a sports marketing agency, while juggling being a first-time mum to her daughter, Fiamma. She is always in need of quick fixes for dinner and has become an expert at fresh and tasty pasta sauces or risottos that can be rustled up from store-cupboard essentials. This lead to her having her own TV series on Channel 4 called Simply Italian and an online blog with her sisters: www.thechiappas.com. She also runs The College House, a coffee and pizza café, in Cardiff, with her husband (see pages 280–83).

EMANUELA (or Emi) is the middle sister, and was often mistaken for Miki's twin when they were growing up; Mum would always dress them identically! However, this is where the similarities end, as Emi is very much a home-bird. Happy with a bucket and spade when she was little, she is now equally content with a pot on the stove or anything hands-on and crafty. She is kept busy juggling her job as a full-time nanny alongside an online business making bespoke gifts for babies. Emi has become an expert in the more time-consuming and technical dishes like fresh filled pasta parcels (for example *Tortelli Piacentini* or *Anolini* on pages 64 and 77) and she loves experimenting with modern twists of traditional recipes.

ROMINA (or Mina) is the youngest of the family and has inherited the family's dark Mediterranean colouring. She is also the only family member to love maths (the rest of us are terrible with numbers) and combining this with a quirky sense of style she currently works at the head office of a luxury fashion label. With two older (louder) sisters, Mina grew up calm and collected, knowing exactly what she wanted and she doesn't do girly fuss or drama. But don't be fooled: behind her cool exterior, Romina has a wild side and is always the first one on the dance floor! Romina has also picked up our Nonno Mauro's secret baking tips and always adds her splash of creativity and individuality to any party we host. So she's the family party planner and baker who loves to entertain. Romina also heads up the wedding business the sisters have set up 'CoHo Italian Weddings', which offers a bespoke service to couples wanting to get married in Italy.

To find out more please visit www.thechiappas.com

Store-Cupboard Essentials

Arborio rice

This is essential for risotto; the grains puff up, absorbing flavour. Most risottos can be cooked in about 20 minutes, making a tasty and quick meal. And they only use one pot.

Balsamic vinegar

Balsamic vinegar is an ever-present ingredient in the Chiappa household. If you need a quick snack, just make some 'pooch' from a little olive oil, balsamic vinegar and salt and use it as a dip for crunchy carrots and celery, or bread and crackers. Our Balsamic Glaze (see page 232) is also really simple to make; keep it to hand for *antipasti* or to drizzle over fresh strawberries.

Olive oil and extra virgin olive oil

Don't ever run out! Use regular olive oil for cooking and extra virgin olive oil for dressings and for drizzling.

Onions and garlic

These form the base for so many Italian recipes. They last a long time and you should always have a ready supply.

Parmesan cheese

Lots of people have asked us how to store Parmesan so it stays fresh. Mum's tip is to grate it and then freeze it immediately in bags. You can use it straight from frozen. Parmesan is too expensive to allow it to become mouldy in your fridge and NEVER buy pre-grated Parmesan, as it's not nearly as good quality.

Dried pasta

Always have a couple of packets of dried spaghetti or linguine and penne or farfalle in your cupboard for impromptu visitors. You can rustle up a great pasta dish with just a few basic ingredients. See our speedy sauces recipes on pages 92–3.

Dried pasta has a very different texture and taste from fresh pasta. However, it is wonderfully easy to store and use, and is more appropriate for certain recipes than fresh pasta. It is much more robust, so can be cooked for longer without becoming mushy. However, we would never, EVER buy ready-made *tortelli* or *ravioli*; only fresh pasta will do here. So, you see, both types of pasta – fresh and dried – have their place. Here are some of our favourite dried pasta shapes and how to use them:

* *Farfalle and penne* – great in classic tomato-based dishes.
* *Mezze-penne* (half-penne) and *conchiglie* (shells) – fantastic in soups and stews (see Nonna's Lentil Pasta Stew on page 221).
* *Pastina* – probably our favourite type of dried pasta comes in many different shapes, and it is a great food to give to babies when they start to eat solids. Add to soups for extra texture. Try it in our Chicken Broth (see page 218).

Pesto

Fresh pesto (see pages 117 and 118) will keep for months in your fridge, provided you cover the top with a layer of olive oil. However, you can also freeze pesto in ice-cube trays. Once frozen, push the pesto cubes in to a freezer bag to save space. When you want a quick pasta dish, simply toss a frozen pesto cube onto your drained cooked pasta and heat for a couple of minutes until it has dissolved and warmed through.

Polenta

We often use instant polenta, as it is ready in less than 10 minutes. Traditional polenta is coarsely ground and takes much longer to cook. For our busy lifestyles, we find instant polenta works just as well. It's also useful when making fresh pasta to stop the dough sticking.

Porcini mushrooms

Dried porcini can be stored for months and are brilliant if you need to make a tasty meal but don't have any fresh ingredients. See our Cheat's Mushroom Risotto recipe on page 136.

Stock cubes

We love home-made stocks and use it whenever we can, but good-quality stock cubes are a great substitute.

Tinned tomatoes

We keep several tins on standby in our cupboards. Turn to page 96 to see how many variations there are on our Classic Tomato Sauce.

Tomato purée

This will keep for ages in your fridge and will help add depth to dishes without overloading on salt.

OUR FREEZER TIPS

Breadcrumbs

If you have leftover bread, allow it to go hard then turn it into breadcrumbs by grating it or whizzing it in a food processor. Keep the breadcrumbs in a bag in the freezer, so they're always on hand.

Frozen spinach

This is usually frozen as soon as it is picked and is packed with nutrients. It's a great vegetable to have stored away to give a boost to a pasta sauce or risotto if you're low on fresh supplies.

Herbs

Are you a sucker for buying fresh herbs from the supermarket, which then die before you've had a chance to use them? Our tip is to finely chop fresh herbs as soon as you buy them and put them into a bag or plastic container in the freezer. You can then use them straight from frozen and this will mean you always have access to fresh herbs. This trick works best with woody herbs such as rosemary and sage.

Individual portions

Miki travels a lot with work and so keeps her freezer stocked with individual meal portions for when she gets home and wants a quick fix for her rumbling tummy. She will often cook bulk supplies at the weekends and divide them into portions for freezing. There is never a need to buy processed foods; create your own home-made ready meals! Gnocchi, tortelli, ravioli, Pasta Pie with Potato Filling, Pasta Pie with Spinach Filling, Aubergine and Mozzarella Bake (see pages 56, 87, 90, 122 and 193) are all great cooked straight from frozen.

Limoncello

This traditional Italian liqueur should always be served ice cold. We like to keep a supply ready in our freezer for any unexpected guests that might arrive!

Raspberries

Raspberries are one of our favourite fruits but they MUST be eaten fresh. If you can't gobble them up immediately, freeze them. Emi needs something sweet after every meal. On the occasions when we don't have a dessert, she knows there will be frozen raspberries in the freezer to munch on.

Wine 'ice cubes'

This is really Romina's tip, as she is the party girl who always has a supply of wine dregs after the weekend! Freeze leftover wine in ice-cube bags or trays and, whenever you need a glass of wine in a recipe, throw in a few frozen wine cubes. This way, you won't have to open a fresh bottle of wine just for cooking.

GREAT ITALIAN INGREDIENTS

Caciotta

Soft and creamy, with a consistency a little like mozzarella but with a saltier taste, this is a delicious melting cheese from our region of Italy, Emilia Romagna. If you can't find caciotta, Taleggio makes a great alternative.

Crodino (or Aperol)

This is a bitter but refreshing drink that is regularly served as an *aperitivo* in Italian bars. A little like a Campari soda, it is bright orange and has an acquired taste, but once you've had it a few times on holiday in Italy, it will bring back lovely memories for the rest of the year.

Funghi stock cubes

Great for adding richness and extra flavour to a porcini sauce or mushroom risotto.

Gutturnio

A chilled sparkling red wine from our region in Italy. Most wine buffs turn their noses up at this, but it's our local wine and we love it! You should certainly try it if you get the chance.

Italian cooked ham

You might think this is the same as any other cooked ham, but it has a taste that reminds us of our Italian summer holidays. Make sure you buy it in wafer-thin slices.

Lievito Pane degli Angeli

Another great Italian ingredient for baking. Its translation means 'Bread of the Angels'. We think it's the 'magic' ingredient to transform certain cake recipes. Essentially it's a sachet of baking powder mixed with vanilla and a little yeast.

Mostarda

A wonderful condiment used traditionally alongside boiled meats. It is made of candied fruit but don't be fooled into thinking it's something sweet as it's coated in a strong mustard syrup so has quite a sweet and fiery combination. An essential and delicious ingredient for our butternut squash wedding tortelli (see page 64).

Ortolina

Just like tomato purée, this will last a long time in your fridge. Made with a combination of veggies (celery, carrots and tomatoes), it is completely delicious and a great addition to a pasta sauce or soup.

Pastina

This is literally 'little pasta', and it comes in lots of different shapes (stars, rings, squares, etc.). We often ate it in soups when we were little and we now love it in a quick broth with lots of Parmesan – all three of us lived on this at university!

Peperoncino

Often used in small amounts in our recipes, not for spice or heat but just enough to give a hint of heat and act as a natural seasoning. Cayenne pepper is a good alternative.

Rio Mare

The ultimate tinned tuna! It is preserved in olive oil and has a distinctive taste that you don't get from tuna in brine or sunflower oil.

Eat Like an Italian

OUR FAVOURITE DISHES FOR DIFFERENT OCCASIONS

PICNIC

Every year, we Welsh-Italians living in South Wales congregate in Abergavenny to celebrate *La Scampagnata* – an Italian gathering. Each family brings car-loads (and even van-loads) of food, and all we do is sit around and visit each other's 'plot', tasting the different recipes and delicacies . . . It's not a competition, but the women secretly compete to cook the best dish! Here we've highlighted some recipes within the book that are perfect for big group and family gathering – dishes that can be easily transported and wrapped up for any foodie picnic:

* Pasta Pie with Potato Filling (page 87)

* Pasta Pie with Spinach Filling (page 90)

* Paola's Pasta Salad or Rice Salad (pages 222, 225)

* Nonno's Mini Sausage Rolls (page 149)

* Crunchy Italian Almond Biscuits (page 279)

* Ultimate Jam Tart (page 272)

SLIMLINE HEALTHY

Eating *all'Italiana* every night does not mean calorie overload. Below are some of our favourite lighter meals which are just as yummy and super healthy:

* Steamed Artichokes with Lemon Salsa (page 25)

* Celery Soup (page 212)

* Bags of Goodness (page 190)

* Stuffed Baked Courgettes (page 203)

* Bean Salad with Tuna and Onion (page 226)

CHILDREN'S FOOD

Being brought up in an Italian household, we were taught to eat the same food as the adults. There was no kids' menu each night for us, but Mum made sure to cook us a feast that both we and our dad would thoroughly enjoy. Our favourite meals as children, which we still enjoy eating today, are highlighted below – recipes that are easy to prepare any day of the week, can be cooked in large quantities and are full of goodness for all the family to enjoy:

* Farfalle with Classic Tomato Sauce (page 96)

* Crispy Polenta with Cheese (page 26)

* Crunchy Breaded Chicken (page 165)

* Pasta Reale in Chicken Broth (page 219)

* Chocolate Gooey Brownies (page 288)

CELEBRATIONS

Our celebratory meals are always filled with plenty of variety, and we'll feast for several hours over endless courses. More often than not we will prepare the dishes ahead of time, as certain special recipes require a little more TLC to get them just right. Below are some suggestions of what we would eat on feast days like Christmas or Easter:

* Anolini (page 77)

* Wedding Tortelli with Butternut Squash (pages 64–6)

* Mum's Braised Beef in Red Wine Stew (page 183)

* Layered Mocha Torte (page 256)

* Puff Pastry with Creamy Mascarpone and Sweet Berries (page 241)

QUICK FIX

The following foods are recipes which we have adapted to suit our busy working lives. Nonna's role in life revolved around the kitchen and feeding her family; night and day she'd be cooking and preparing food. Having full-time jobs means there's not much time to spend in the kitchen, but we like to enjoy home-cooked tasty food, so here is a list of recipes that are quick and easy to prepare after a long day in the office:

* **Zesty Spring Vegetables** (perfect in the summer months, when lots of fresh delicious veg are available) (page 112)

* **Risotto** (20 minutes to make a meal, and cooked in one pot!) (pages 130–39)

* **Lemon Chicken** (page 169)

* **Ice Cream Drowned in Coffee** (page 244)

* **Hot Strawberries with Ice Cream and Amaretti** (page 238)

DINNER PARTY

Entertaining for friends and family can be stressful when you have run out of inspiration for what to cook. We always stick to four courses: *antipasto*, *primo* (pasta), *secondo* (main) and dessert. We like to prepare our food for a dinner party in advance so that we can focus on being glamorous hosts rather than slaving over the stove when the guests arrive. Here is a suggestion of a menu for a dinner party that will always impress and will ensure nobody leaves your home feeling hungry:

* **Preserved Mushrooms** (page 35)

* **Bruschetta** (pages 32–3)

* **Classic Pancakes Stuffed with Spinach and Ricotta** (page 195)

* **Aubergine and Mozzarella Bake** (page 193)

* **Elsa's Chocolate and Biscuit Dessert** (page 249)

* **Tiramisù** (page 250)

RECIPE FLAGS

We have matched every recipe to a different category for you to find your way around this book super speedily if you're looking for something specific. Therefore if you fancy something you can pre-prepare then flick through and look for the 'Get Ahead' yellow flags in the book. If you want a veggie dish, flick through and find the green flags. For each recipe we chose the most appropriate flag, so don't assume there are only a small handful of veggie/freezable dishes . . . many recipes could have had multiple flags, but to keep things simple, we chose the one that we felt worked best for each dish.

A Classic

Freeze

Get Ahead

Get the Kids Involved

Healthy

Something Special

Speedy

Veggie

Antipasti

At about 5 p.m. (or sometimes midday at the weekend, pre-lunch), you'll find Italians enjoying an *aperitivo* in a bar. An *aperitivo* is a pre-dinner drink served with a selection of light nibbles, *antipasti,* designed to 'open' the palate. It also provides an opportunity to relax and socialize while eating a little snack.

A typical drink for an *aperitivo* is prosecco (bubbles!) or a Crodino or Aperol spritz (a bright orange drink a little like a Campari soda). In the summer, Bellinis are also popular (fresh peach juice and prosecco). Most bars will serve your *aperitivo* with some nuts, olives, mini focaccia or a small bowl of crisps.

Milan is a city well known for its *aperitivi* culture and it has taken the notion of 'nibbles' to another level. Locals will often head to a bar after work and order an *aperitivo* or a cocktail. They will then help themselves to the vast selection of antipasti on display – mini mozzarella balls, *fritto misto*, stuffed sun-blushed tomatoes, crispy polenta . . . the list goes on! When Miki worked in Milan during her year abroad at university, she hunted out all the best places (see our suggestions on page 295). As you can probably guess, she was a fan of the 'extended' *aperitivi* and often skipped dinner.

In Italian, '*antipasto*' translates as 'before your meal' and it is the equivalent of a British starter. In a traditional trattoria, so many delicious antipasti can be served that we often don't have enough room for the other courses! Antipasti can vary: they can be hot or cold, seafood or meat – where we are from it is traditional to serve plates of cured meats such as *salame*, *coppa*, *prosciutto crudo*, *culatello* and *mortadella* with bread or *torta fritta* and pickled sweet onions and mushrooms (see pages 34 and 35).

At Casa Chiappa, whenever guests arrive, Mum always has some treats to hand to enjoy with a glass of wine as an *aperitivo* or to create a quick antipasto. It doesn't have to be complicated: hand-torn pieces of toasted bread or focaccia dipped in an olive oil, balsamic vinegar and salt dressing; chunks of Parmesan with Italian meats; or Gorgonzola with crackers and honey.

In this chapter we've collected together recipes for some of our favourite antipasti so you can join in on the Italian fun! Romina often has these as canapés before her dinner parties, although they're just as good on a buffet table. Give them a try so you can see how easy and delicious they are.

Steamed Artichokes with Lemon Salsa

CARCIOFI CLASSICI CON SALSA DI LIMONE

This is the perfect snack to keep you going while you're waiting for your next meal. As kids, it was so much fun picking off the leaves from the artichoke and dipping them in the sauce – little did we know that we were actually eating a vegetable! It's a great snack to share as a family, gathered around the table.

Serves: 3–4
Preparation time: 10 minutes
Cooking time: 30 minutes

2 fresh whole globe artichokes

2 tablespoons olive oil

juice of 1 lemon

fine salt and freshly ground black pepper

4 tablespoons cream cheese

Using a pair of scissors, cut off about 1cm from the tip of each artichoke leaf. Remove the stalks with a sharp knife. Drizzle each artichoke with half a tablespoon of oil and a quarter of the lemon juice, then season with salt and pepper.

Put 250ml water in a large saucepan and bring to the boil over a medium heat. Place the artichokes in the pan, with their bases resting on the bottom. Cover with a lid and steam for 30 minutes. Keep an eye on the water and top up if necessary. To check the artichokes are cooked, carefully turn them over and press the base; if your finger leaves an indentation, then they are ready. Be careful not to burn yourself.

Meanwhile, in a small bowl, whisk together the cream cheese, the remaining lemon juice and the remaining oil. Season with salt and pepper and mix to combine.

We like to serve this on a big chopping board in the middle of the table so that everyone can get stuck in.

 TIPS

Try adding a little chilli or cayenne pepper to the lemon salsa to give it some extra kick.

If the lemon salsa is too sharp, stir through some more cream cheese.

Crispy Polenta with Cheese

POLENTA CROCCANTE AL FORMAGGIO

Such a treat! When we were little, Mum would always make extra polenta and leave it to cool in the fridge. For dinner the next night she would slice it and fry it until crispy, with melted cheese on top. Sometimes she'd cut it into chunky strips before frying, which we loved to eat as an afternoon snack, or served alongside a little breaded veal or chicken.

Serves: 4–6
Preparation time: 15 minutes
Chilling time: 20 minutes,
or overnight
Cooking time: 30 minutes

150g instant polenta

50g salted butter

250g caciotta cheese

optional: Balsamic Glaze
(see page 232), to drizzle

fine salt

Prepare the polenta according to the packet instructions, whisking until thoroughly mixed and smooth. The polenta should be quite thick, but don't worry: it will make it easier to slice.

Pour the polenta into a loaf tin and leave to cool, then chill in the fridge for at least 20 minutes, or overnight.

When the polenta has completely cooled, turn it out onto a chopping board. Cut into 1.5cm slices, as though slicing a loaf of bread.

Over a medium heat, melt the butter in a frying pan. Fry the polenta slices for 5 minutes on each side, until they crisp up. Keep the polenta on the heat for longer than you might expect to get a real crispy texture.

Slice the cheese and place on top of the polenta. (If you want the cheese properly melted, place under a hot grill for a few minutes.) Serve drizzled with a little balsamic glaze.

⊗ TIPS

You can use different cheeses to top the polenta - try Cheddar, Gorgonzola or mozzarella. Romina loves to make this with halloumi, which you should fry in a separate pan, as it doesn't melt like other cheeses.

Add a few rosemary leaves to the pan when you fry the polenta for some extra flavour.

Try using a sweet chilli sauce instead of the balsamic glaze.

Beer-Battered Crispy Seafood

FRITTO MISTO

This dish takes us back to the seaside town of Santa Margherita in Liguria. We often drove down from the mountain to spend a few days at the beach and this was always Dad's first choice on the menu. However, we're lucky enough to be able to enjoy it in Wales, too! On a Saturday night, you'll often find us piled into one of Dad's delivery vans on the way to Porthcawl to visit our Italian–Welsh friends, the Sidolis. They own a number of fish-and-chip bars and they'll sometimes have a lock-in just for us. They'll cook us fresh calamari with chips – and we usually take a few bottles of Peroni or prosecco.

Serves: 4
Preparation time: 15 minutes
Chilling time: 10 minutes
Cooking time: 10 minutes

150g Tipo '00' flour, plus extra to dust

100ml beer

150ml cold sparkling water

200g raw prawns, heads removed, tails left on (if frozen, make sure they're fully defrosted)

200g baby squid, prepared, cleaned and sliced into 1cm rings

120g whitebait

fine salt and freshly ground black pepper

vegetable oil, for deep-fat frying

wedges of lemon, to serve

Mix the flour, beer and water in a bowl until it forms a batter, then chill in the fridge for 10 minutes.

Meanwhile, wash all the seafood with cold water and pat dry with some kitchen paper. Season with salt and pepper, and dust all over with flour.

Pour the oil into a large pan to a depth of about 8cm. Heat the oil until a small piece of batter dropped in bubbles and quickly turns golden brown. One at a time, dip the pieces of seafood in the batter and lower straight into the hot oil. Fry about 10 pieces at a time, for 3 minutes on each side, until crispy – take care not to burn them. Do not overcrowd the pan, as the seafood won't cook properly. Repeat with the rest.

Use a slotted spoon to remove the pieces from the oil and drain on kitchen paper. Serve immediately with wedges of lemon and sprinkled with salt.

 TIP

We recommend cooking this dish outside, if possible, or at least opening lots of windows, as it can make your kitchen rather smelly!

Bruschetta

Everyone loves a traditional bruschetta and we'll often whip the classic tomato one together as a pre-dinner snack. However, we've also given an extra two ideas for toppings here; a zingy celery and lime version followed by a vibrant pea and mint. Any of these are perfect for serving at parties. And we also love that, if served together, they make up the red, white and green of the Italian flag! Make sure your bread is well toasted and crispy so it absorbs the juices of the topping without going soggy. There's nothing worse than soggy bruschetta.

For each recipe, begin by toasting ciabatta or baguette slices until golden. (You can do this using a toaster, or drizzle the bread with a little olive oil and brown in a pan over a medium heat). For extra crisp bread, leave the toasted slices exposed to the air to harden for a day or two before using.

CLASSIC TOMATO BRUSCHETTA

Bruschetta Rossa

Romina always makes these when she has a house party, as they look pretty and are good finger food, although sometimes the garlic isn't welcomed . . .

Serves: 6
Preparation time: 5 minutes
Chilling time: 20 minutes,
or overnight
Cooking time: 5 minutes

300g fresh tomatoes
(approx. 3 large beef tomatoes)

2 garlic cloves, crushed

8 fresh basil leaves, plus
extra to garnish

3 tablespoons extra virgin
olive oil, plus extra to drizzle
if needed

fine salt and freshly ground
black pepper

6 thick slices of ciabatta
or baguette

Chop the tomatoes into small chunks and place in a bowl with all their juices.

Add the garlic to the bowl with the tomato flesh. Tear the 8 basil leaves into small pieces and add to the bowl along with the oil. Stir together and season with salt and pepper. Marinate in the fridge for at least 20 minutes, or longer, if possible.

Spread each slice of bread with a tablespoon of the tomato mixture and garnish with a few basil leaves.

 TIPS

Try drizzling with a little Classic Pesto or Balsamic Glaze (see page 117 or 232).

In some regions of Italy it is traditional to rub a clove of raw garlic over the bread before adding the topping.

GARLIC, CELERY AND LIME BRUSCHETTA

Bruschetta Fresca

You might think celery bruschetta sounds a bit strange, but trust us. This is a really refreshing and tasty *aperitivo* – especially if you have some last-minute guests!

Serves: 6
Preparation time: 5 minutes
Cooking time: 5 minutes

4 large sticks of celery

1–2 garlic cloves, peeled

6 tablespoons extra virgin olive oil, plus extra to drizzle if needed

juice of ½ a lime

fine salt and freshly ground black pepper

6 thick slices of ciabatta or baguette

Put 3 sticks of celery and the garlic in a food processor and blend to a purée. Scrape into a bowl. Finely chop the remaining stick of celery and leave to one side.

Add the oil and lime juice to the puréed celery. Season, to taste, with salt and pepper and stir together to combine.

Spread each slice of bread with a tablespoon of the celery mixture and garnish with a sprinkling of the finely chopped celery.

 TIP

Keep the celery in the fridge so that it's nice and cold before using; it makes a lovely fresh contrast to the warm bread.

PEA BRUSCHETTA WITH BUFFALO MOZZARELLA

Bruschetta Verde

Emi discovered this combination of flavours while on her honeymoon in southern Tuscany.

Serves: 6
Preparation time: 5 minutes
Cooking time: 10 minutes

250g peas

8 fresh mint leaves

1 teaspoon extra virgin olive oil, plus extra to drizzle if needed

fine salt and freshly ground black pepper

2 tablespoons Salsa Verde (see page 232), plus extra to drizzle

6 thick slices of ciabatta or baguette

125g buffalo mozzarella

Put half the peas and all the mint in a food processor and blend to a purée. Scrape into a bowl. Add the remaining whole peas, the oil, a little salt and pepper, and the salsa verde. Mix well to combine.

Spread each slice of bread with a tablespoon of the pea mixture. Tear the mozzarella with your hands and arrange on top. Sprinkle with a little more salt and pepper, to taste. Place the bruschettas on a baking tray and grill for 1 or 2 minutes, until the cheese has melted.

Drizzle with a little extra Salsa Verde, Classic Pesto or Balsamic Glaze (see pages 117 and 232) just before serving.

Sweet Balsamic Onions from Monte Vacà

CIPOLLINE DI MONTE VACÀ

These onions are one of the reasons we go running back to the mountain trattoria, Monte Vacà, every summer. They're just so sweet and juicy, none of us can resist them. They're usually served alongside Preserved Mushrooms (see opposite) or a selection of Italian hams and cured meats.

Serves: 3–4
Preparation time: 10 minutes
Cooking time: 10 minutes

350ml white wine vinegar

50ml balsamic vinegar

2 tablespoons brown sugar

300g button onions, peeled

1 tablespoon olive oil, plus extra to cover

a pinch of salt

First, sterilize the jar that you are going to use (see below). It needs to be a 370g jar.

In a small saucepan, bring the vinegars, brown sugar and 100ml water to the boil. Add the onions, reduce the heat and simmer for 5 minutes. Reserving the vinaigrette, remove the onions and pat dry with paper towels.

Heat the oil in a frying pan over a medium heat and fry the onions for about 5 minutes, stirring, until golden all over. Season with salt.

Pack the onions into the sterilized jar and cover with one third of the vinaigrette. Cover with more oil.

STERILIZING A JAR

To sterilize a jar or bottle, preheat the oven to 180°C/350°F/gas 4.

Wash the jar or bottle (and lid) in hot soapy water. Rinse well and dry thoroughly with a clean tea towel.

Place on a baking tray and put in the oven for about 5 minutes.

Place your contents into the jar and seal.

Preserved Mushrooms

FUNGHI SOTT OLIO

We usually make a few jars of these so we're well stocked for the Christmas party season. Baby porcini mushrooms also work really well here (use fresh rather than dried) or try experimenting with unusual varieties – you don't have to use button mushrooms. Cut any large mushrooms into bite-sized pieces.

Serves: 6–8
Preparation time: 10 minutes
Cooking time: 10 minutes

350ml white wine vinegar

1 garlic clove, peeled

1 teaspoon fine salt

4 black peppercorns

2 cloves

optional: 4 cloves of garlic

500g button mushrooms, thoroughly cleaned to remove all traces of earth

olive oil, to cover

If you are going to store these, sterilize the jar that you're going to keep the mushrooms in (see opposite). It needs to hold about 450ml.

In a frying pan, bring the vinegar and 100ml water to the boil. Add the garlic, salt, peppercorns, cloves, the extra garlic (if using) and the mushrooms, then simmer for 10 minutes.

Remove the mushrooms and leave to drain on some kitchen paper. Be careful not to touch them with your hands if you are planning on storing them, to avoid transferring any bacteria to them.

Pour a little oil into the bottom of the cooled sterilized jar. Spoon in the mushrooms, packing them in tightly so there is no trapped air. Cover with more oil. If you like, you can add the peppercorns, cloves and garlic to the jar for extra flavour.

Pasta

'*Pasta*' in Italian literally translates as 'dough', but to us Brits, pasta is simply pasta. Most Italians will break for an hour at lunch to eat a plate of pasta; it's the heart and soul of Italian cooking, the building blocks of a nation. Everyone, from high society to truck drivers, will take time out at lunch to sit down and savour a good meal – it's rarely a sandwich on the go.

In this section, we're introducing you to the world of **fresh pasta**. People often think that making fresh pasta is very difficult, but it's actually very simple: it's just flour and eggs! We learned how to make pasta from Nonna Luisa and Mum and it really is just down to practice. It can be a little bit unpredictable because so much depends on the type of flour, the size of the eggs and even the weather, but it's important for the dough to achieve the right consistency. We've included lots of helpful tips to help you along the way. We'll also introduce you to different shapes and colours of pasta, and a multitude of sauces to go with each one.

A **pasta sauce** can be one of the quickest things you'll ever make. We're amazed that people buy ready-made pasta sauces when they are so simple to throw together.

Nowadays, everyone seems to be running against the clock, so we've given you a selection of super-quick, speedy sauces, as well as some more adventurous options. But be creative and keep experimenting until you find the taste you're looking for. If you have some meat or vegetables that need eating up, start with the Classic Tomato Sauce (see page 96) and add whatever you have to hand – before you know it, you'll have a truly original, delicious pasta sauce. And what's even better is that while you're waiting for the water to boil for the pasta, you can cook your sauce, so everything is timed to perfection.

The sauces in this chapter can be mixed-and-matched with most types of pasta. As a rough guide, though, meatier and heavier sauces (such as our Bolognese on page 102) go best with a wide pasta such as pappardelle or tagliatelle, whereas lighter, fresher sauces (like Mum's Summer Chilled Tomato Sauce on page 100) work well with delicate pastas like *spaghetti* and *linguine*.

When it comes to **filled pasta** (*tortelli*, *ravioli*, etc.) don't cut corners and buy a readymade version; fresh is a completely different – and far superior – experience. From the minute we could walk and talk we were pulled into the kitchen to help in the production line making fresh filled pasta: one of us on the pasta roller, another filling, and the third sealing and cutting. Emilia Romagna, where our family is from in Italy, is known as the capital of filled pasta, and you'll find a whole range of shapes available across the region. Italians love a debate and every town, village and even family will have their own opinion on what is the 'right' way to make *tortelli*. See page 57 for ours.

Baked pasta is where you'll find Traditional Lasagne (see page 78) as well as our Green Lasagne made with sage and walnut pesto and mozzarella (see page 80). But baked pasta doesn't stop here, oh no! We've given you the recipe for *nidi*, which are little fresh-pasta 'nests' made with a variety of fillings (see page 83), and also pasta pies (see page 87–91). These can be found in local bakeries throughout northern Italy, with each village serving a variety unique to that area.

Pasta Notes

MAKING FRESH PASTA

* Always keep fresh pasta dough covered with cling film, otherwise it will start to go dry and form a crust if exposed to air, and it will be difficult to roll.

* Make sure there is a light dusting of flour on your work surface to prevent the pasta from sticking.

* Once you've made your pasta shapes, leave them to rest on a tray that has been lightly dusted with a little polenta or semolina. Don't use flour to dust the tray, as too much flour will make your pasta heavy.

* If you're making fresh filled pasta parcels in a production line, and the person on the pasta roller is moving too quickly for the fillers and cutters to keep up, lay out the pasta sheets individually under cling film so that they don't stick together or dry out before cutting. You want to keep your pasta soft until you've filled and sealed your parcels.

* If you are making a spaghetti-style pasta (e.g. linguine, tagliatelle or pappardelle) it can help to hang the pasta sheets on clean coat hangers or a wire clothes rack to air-dry for about 20 minutes before cutting.

* If you make more fresh pasta than you need, leave it to air-dry in a warm, dry place for 2 or 3 days. Rotate it to make sure it dries evenly. When it is completely dry, store in airtight jars and it will keep for several months.

TIPS

Cup: Find a cup that can measure out 100g flour, so you won't have to weigh it each time.

Flour: You should ideally use Tipo '00' flour to make fresh pasta. It makes a world of difference. Don't make life difficult; invest in good-quality flour.

Eggs: You can use any medium-sized eggs but the better the quality of the egg, the better the dough. In Italy they use eggs with a large and very yellow yolk, which gives the pasta a vibrant yellow colour. Try corn-fed chicken's eggs for a similar effect.

Cling film: Always cover the dough with cling film while it's resting, otherwise it can harden and form a crust.

Resting: You don't always need to rest the dough; we know what it's like to be in a rush (or if you're Miki, just hungry!) so by all means use your dough straight away. BUT if you do have time for it to rest even for 15 minutes (after all, we all like a little coffee break!) it will really help your pasta achieve the elasticity it needs.

Washing up: If your surfaces have lots of flour on them, don't wipe them with a wet dishcloth. FLOUR + WATER = A STICKY MESS! Our Mum used to go mad if we wiped up a load of flour with her clean dishcloths. Instead, use anything with a firm flat edge (a plastic scraper or the back edge of a blunt knife) to scrape off the excess flour, and then wipe the remains with kitchen paper.

THE DOUGH

The Basic Egg Pasta recipe on page 40 is easy and doesn't change. What does change is the quality of the flour, the size of the eggs and the humidity of the air (think about how your hair reacts differently when you wash it on a wet day). Don't panic! What is important is to know what consistency you are trying to achieve, then you can adjust the ingredients accordingly.

The consistency of pasta dough should be like Play-doh; it shouldn't be too dry or fall apart but nor should it be too wet and stick to your hands. To help you achieve the right consistency try the following:

* To help prevent the dough from being too wet, hold back the last egg if you are using more than 100g flour. Add the final egg slowly, yolk first, and then the white. You might not need the final egg at all, or maybe only the yolk.

* If it is still too wet and sticking to your hands, add a little more flour until it binds. But don't be tempted to add too much flour; the more flour you add, the heavier the pasta. When flour comes into contact with water it becomes sticky because of the starch. If you add too much flour, your pasta will become claggy and stodgy. (This is why you should always place finished pasta shapes on a tray dusted with polenta or semolina, rather than flour.)

* If the dough is too dry (i.e. completely falling apart and not binding at all) mix in a teaspoon of olive oil. But only do this IF ABSOLUTELY NECESSARY — it's fine if it's a little dry and crumbly as it will firm up as it rests.

COOKING PASTA

* Make sure you have at least two-thirds more water than pasta in the pan.

* Always salt your water; it should taste like sea water.

* Fresh pasta cooks much quicker than dried.

* Taste your pasta before draining it – don't worry too much about following the timing instructions on the packet. *Al dente* means 'with a bite', so you want the pasta to be cooked and soft with a little bite to it.

* Always mix the pasta and sauce over a low heat. Never put the pasta in a bowl and then put your sauce on top to serve, as it won't combine as well and you will end up eating chunks of plain bland pasta – plus if you don't add some moisture to the cooked pasta it will stick together in clumps. Not nice!

* Never drown your pasta in sauce. The pasta should just be coated, not swimming in a soup.

* Use 2 or 3 tablespoons of the pasta cooking water to help it mix with the sauce.

Basic Egg Pasta Dough

LA PASTA

The recipe below uses 100g flour, which will make enough pasta for 1 or 2 people. If cooking for more, the quantities are easy to multiply. Here are our suggested serving amounts: Pasta dough made with 100g flour + 1 egg will make enough pasta for 1–2 people; Pasta dough made with 200g flour + 2 eggs will make enough pasta for 2–3 people; Pasta dough made with 400g flour + 4 eggs will make enough pasta for 4–6 people.

Serves: 1–2
Preparation time: 10 minutes
Resting time: 30 minutes

100g Tipo '00' flour, plus extra if needed

1 medium egg, preferably free-range or organic

fine salt

1 teaspoon olive oil, if needed

Place the flour on a board or in a large bowl and make a well in the centre. Crack the egg into the well and add a pinch of salt. Using a fork, gradually mix the egg into the flour. Don't worry if there are lumps in the dough at this stage. Keep mixing until crumbs form, then place the dough on a flat surface. (You can speed up this process by mixing the ingredients in a food processor until they bind.)

Knead the dough until it is silky, smooth and elastic. If the dough is crumbly (too dry) add a little olive oil; if the dough sticks to your hands (too wet) add a little extra flour. Cover with cling film and rest for 30 minutes at room temperature. If you don't want to cut your pasta immediately, you can keep the dough in the fridge overnight. However, if you leave it any longer, you risk the dough turning black.

Gluten-Free Basic Egg Pasta Dough

PASTA SENZA GLUTINE

A lot of people ask us how to make gluten-free pasta and whether they can just substitute normal flour with gluten-free flour. Unfortunately, it's not that simple. Gluten is the binding agent, which gives the dough its elasticity. However, after lots of experimenting, we've found a solution! This recipe results in delicious pasta every time – we urge you to try it to see if you can tell the difference. It's quite amazing and hopefully will be a success with any gluten-free people out there. You can shape the dough just like regular dough, although it may need a few more turns through the pasta roller (see Tips).

Serves: 3–4
Preparation time: 10 minutes
Resting time: 30 minutes

100g rice flour, plus extra to dust

100g corn starch or cornflour

3 tablespoons potato flour

2 teaspoons Xanthan gum

fine salt

3 medium eggs, preferably free-range or organic

1½ tablespoons olive oil

Put the rice flour, corn starch, potato flour, Xanthan gum and a pinch of salt in a food processor, and pulse to mix. Add the eggs and oil and blitz until well combined. You can also do this by hand.

Tip onto a flat surface dusted with a little rice flour, and knead gently to form a dough. Cover with cling film and rest for 30 minutes at room temperature.

⊗ TIPS

When rolling the pasta dough, use the same method as for rolling regular pasta dough (see page 48) but be aware that it might be a bit crumbly because there isn't any gluten in the flour. Do not fret! Patch the pieces together gently and push the dough through the pasta roller on its widest setting again. Keep persisting, patching the pieces and working with the dough and rolling it through, until the dough comes out in one piece. Just have a little patience.

Xanthan gum acts as a substitute for gluten and helps bind the flours. You can find xanthan gum, rice flour and potato flour in most major supermarkets, usually located in the gluten-free aisle.

Coloured Pasta Dough

Colouring pasta doesn't really change its taste but it is really pretty stored in jars in the kitchen and can makes dishes look very dramatic!

Coloured pasta cooks incredibly quickly; if you cook it from fresh it can sometimes take just 10 seconds! And beetroot pasta can be cooked in just 5 seconds! Taste, taste, taste to check it is cooked and as soon as it is *al dente*, pull it out of the water. Cooking the pasta will bleach out some of the colour, so don't worry if the pasta ends up a little paler than expected (this is especially true of beetroot pasta). Leaving the cut pasta to dry overnight (see page 38) will help it to retain its colour.

GREEN PASTA

The spinach in this recipe hardly makes any difference to the taste of the pasta, but it turns the dough a fantastic, vibrant green, making it hard for anyone to resist. It's a great way to get kids to eat their greens.

Serves: 4–6
Preparation time: 20 minutes
Resting time: 30 minutes

235g spinach leaves, washed and patted dry

400g Tipo '00' flour, plus extra to dust

2 medium eggs, preferably free-range or organic

fine salt

Steam the spinach in a large covered saucepan, with a little water, for about 5 minutes, until the spinach has wilted. Remove from the heat, drain and leave to cool (you can speed up the cooling process by running cold water over the spinach).

When the spinach is cool enough to handle, squeeze to remove all the water. This is a really important step. If there's any excess water in the filling it may cause the pasta to disintegrate, so make sure the spinach is as dry as possible.

Finely chop the spinach, running the knife over the top from time to time to create a paste. (To speed up this process blitz the spinach in a food processor.)

Put the flour, 2 eggs, a pinch of salt and the spinach in a large bowl. Mix well to combine.

Once the dough has come together, transfer to a lightly floured surface and knead until it has the consistency of Play-doh. Cover with cling film and rest for 30 minutes at room temperature.

eggs+flour=   eggs+flour+spinach=

basic egg pasta   green pasta

eggs+flour+beetroot=   eggs+flour+tomato purée=

pink pasta   orange pasta

ORANGE PASTA

This is a very simple but effective way to colour pasta.

Serves: 4–6
Preparation time: 10 minutes
Resting time: 30 minutes

2 tablespoons tomato purée

2–3 medium eggs, preferably free-range or organic

400g Tipo '00' flour, plus extra to dust

fine salt

Mix the tomato purée with the eggs and continue with the Basic Egg Pasta Dough recipe method (see page 40).

BLACK PASTA

This is very striking and is fantastic used in seafood recipes. It will also make a great contrast to the other colours of pasta in your kitchen.

Serves: 4–6
Preparation time: 10 minutes
Resting time: 30 minutes

1 x 5g sachet of squid ink

3–4 medium eggs, preferably free-range or organic

400g Tipo '00' flour, plus extra to dust

fine salt

Mix the squid ink into the eggs and whisk to combine. Continue with the Basic Egg Pasta Dough recipe method (see page 40). You may find that you need to use a little extra flour.

PINK PASTA

We LOVE to prepare beetroot pasta, if only because it looks like a massive ball of bubble-gum! You can use bought pre-cooked beetroot but make sure it's not the kind that's in vinegar.

Serves: 2
Preparation time: 15 minutes
Resting time: 30 minutes

75g cooked beetroot, cooled completely

1 medium egg, preferably free-range or organic

fine salt

200g Tipo '00' flour, plus extra to dust

Blend the beetroot in a food processor until you have a rough paste. Add the egg and a pinch of salt, and blitz to a smooth purée.

Place the flour in a large mixing bowl and create a well in the centre. Pour in the pink purée and mix with a fork to form a dough. (You can speed up this process by mixing your ingredients in a food processor until they bind.) When crumbs start to form, continue with the Basic Egg Pasta Dough (see page 40) This dough is often very sticky because of the moisture from the beetroot, so add extra flour if necessary and knead until the dough stops sticking to your hands (see page 39).

Rolling the Dough

Before you make any shape of pasta, you need to roll your dough into long, thin sheets. If your dough has a good elastic consistency, you shouldn't need much extra flour for this stage.

1. When the dough has rested, take a tennis-ball-sized amount and squash it flat with your fingers. (Always keep the rest of the dough covered with cling film so it doesn't dry out and form a crust.)

2. With the pasta roller set to its widest setting, roll the dough through. If the dough is too sticky to go through smoothly, dust both sides with a little flour and try again. Try to avoid using too much flour, though, otherwise the pasta will feel heavy and claggy when it is cooked. Once it rolls through smoothly, fold into thirds, and repeat this step 3 times.

3. When the dough has formed a rough square shape, start working it through the machine, taking it down one setting at a time, until you reach the last and thinnest setting. Dust with a little more flour as you go, if you need to. Repeat with the rest of the dough. (You can also roll the dough by hand using a rolling pin, but you'll need some serious elbow grease to get your pasta sheets nice and thin.)

4. You will end up with long rectangular sheets of pasta approximately 8–10cm wide and about the thickness of 2 playing cards. Lightly dust a flat surface with polenta or semolina and lay out the pasta sheets.

From these sheets, you can create different shapes of pasta: lasagne, linguine, tagliatelle, pappardelle, ravioli and tortelli, farfalle . . .

Always cover the dough with cling film while it is resting so that it doesn't harden or form a crust.

Shaping the Dough

Learning to make different shapes from pasta dough is great fun and we have fond memories of doing this with Nonna Luisa and Mum. It's how we learned to cook. We often spend a rainy Welsh weekend making massive batches of pasta in different shapes and colours.

Of course, there are hundreds of different pasta shapes – Italians love to have their own opinions on the best way to do things! Different regions will often have the same type of pasta but will give it a completely different name. For example, what we call tortelli in Parma are called tortellini or ravioli in Bologna. Similarly, there are lots of different names for pappardelle, depending on whether it has crinkled or straight edges. What we've tried to do is introduce you to some of the basic pasta shapes but ultimately you can experiment and try lots of different shapes and colours – have fun with it!

Before you create any of the following pasta shapes, you'll need to roll a long, thin sheet of pasta (see page 48).

LASAGNE SHEETS

These are wide sheets of pasta that are very easy to make, as you don't need to do much to your lasagne sheet once it's been rolled out. If you're planning on making lasagne (see pages 78 or 80), aim to cut the pasta strips to be at least the length of your ovenproof dish to make layering easier. The lasagne strips can be prepared several hours in advance. Lay them on a tray that has been lightly dusted with polenta to stop them sticking together, ensuring they don't overlap, and cover them in cling film so they don't dry out.

LINGUINE

This is like flat spaghetti and suits light, delicate sauces.

Sprinkle a little flour over both sides of the pasta sheet and fold it into thirds (short edges together). Using a sharp knife, cut into 3mm-wide strips, lengthways. When you unfold the pasta you will have long linguine.

TAGLIATELLE

This is the middle ground between linguine and pappardelle.

Sprinkle a little flour over both sides of the pasta sheet and fold it into thirds (short edges together). Using a sharp knife, cut into 1cm-wide strips, lengthways. When you unfold the pasta you will have long tagliatelle.

PAPPARDELLE

Wide, long strips of pasta – great with heavier or meaty sauces.

Sprinkle a little flour over both sides of the pasta sheet and fold it into thirds (short edges together). Trim the long edges straight with a sharp knife, and cut into 2.5cm-wide strips, lengthways. When you unfold the pasta you will have long pappardelle.

PREPARING THE PASTA SHAPES

Once you have made each pasta shape, place it on a tray which has been dusted with a little polenta or semolina. It's important that the shapes don't touch until they have air-dried for at least 20 minutes, as they might not hold their shape or they could stick together. If you are making long strips of pasta (e.g. linguine, tagliatelle or pappardelle), hang them on clean coat hangers or a wire clothes rack for 10–15 minutes after cutting.

FARFALLE

Children love farfalle (which means 'butterflies' in Italian), and they go very well with Oozy Tomato Sauce (see page 99).

Place a sheet of pasta on a lightly floured surface. Using a pasta-cutting wheel or sharp knife, cut your pasta into strips roughly 3–4cm wide, then cut across these to create little rectangles about the size of small matchboxes.

Take each pasta rectangle and, with dry or lightly floured fingers, pinch in the middle to create a butterfly shape. If your pasta is too dry, wet your fingertips with a little water to help the sides stick together. Place the farfalle in orderly rows on trays that have been lightly dusted with polenta or semolina, and repeat the process until you have used all the remaining dough. Leave to air-dry for 20 minutes so that they hold their shape while cooking.

SILHOUETTE PASTA WITH HERBS

This is pappardelle with herbs running through it. You will need a big bunch of fresh herbs such as basil, parsley or chervil. Ideally choose a bunch with smaller leaves, as these will produce prettier, more delicate pasta.

Lay a pasta sheet lengthways on a floured surface and spritz half of it with water. Place individual herb leaves in lines along the length of the damp pasta leaving about 1cm between each line.

Spritz the other half of the pasta sheet with water and fold it over to cover the herbs. Press down gently to help seal the two layers together then dust the top of the pasta with a little semolina. Using a rolling pin, gently roll over the pasta to fully seal the two layers together, and make the pasta a little thinner. Be careful not to press too hard, as you could bruise the leaves.

Fold into thirds (short edges together). Trim the long edges straight with a sharp knife and then cut between the lines of herbs into long 2.5cm-wide strips. Unfold the pasta and place on trays lightly dusted with polenta or semolina, or hang on clean coat hangers or a wire clothes rack, and leave to air-dry for 20 minutes before cooking.

Filled Pasta

You simply cannot compare fresh, homemade ravioli or tortelli with their shop-bought counterparts. They taste completely different – like a totally different dish! Be creative with your fillings, but make sure they're not too wet, as the moisture can soak into the pasta and it may collapse as it cooks. See pages 60 and 61 for some of our favourite fillings. Don't let the ravioli sit for too long once you've made them, as the filling can soak into the pasta and cause it to disintegrate. Either cook them straight away, or put them in the freezer, still on their trays, for 2 to 3 hours. Once frozen, you can transfer them to freezer bags. They can be cooked from frozen, although they may take a little longer, so always taste one to check they are cooked before serving.

Before you make filled pasta parcels, you first need to roll a long, thin sheet of pasta (see page 48).

1. Place a sheet of pasta on a lightly floured surface and cut it in half lengthways.

2. Using a pasta-cutter, a knife or a biscuit cutter, lightly mark out on the bottom pasta sheet where you want to cut the shapes.

3. Spoon about a teaspoon of filling into the centre of each shape; you ideally want to leave 1cm of pasta around the edge of the filling.

4. Dip your finger in water, and trace the pasta around the filling. This will help the top layer of pasta stick. (You could also spray water onto the pasta.)

5. Carefully lay the top pasta sheet half over the sheet with the filling. Using your fingers, press around the filling to squeeze out any air and completely seal the two layers together. It's important that the pasta parcels are completely sealed with no air pockets so they don't burst open as they cook.

6. Cut the pasta parcels to your chosen shape using the cutter or a sharp knife, resting each parcel on a tray lightly dusted with polenta or semolina as you go. Make sure they aren't touching, as they could stick together.

7. Bring a large pan of salted water to the boil. Carefully place the pasta parcels in the boiling water and cook for 3 minutes. Don't let the water boil too vigorously as this may cause them to split. Always taste one to check they are cooked before serving.

 TIP

Gather together any off-cuts of pasta and use them to make some more pasta parcels. Knead the dough with a little oil or water if it's a bit dry.

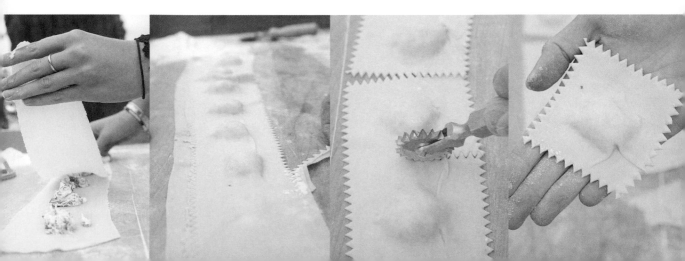

ANOLINI

Anolini are similar to ravioli and tortelli but they are much smaller and have very little pasta around their edges – they are more like dumplings. To make them, you ideally need a small circular pasta cutter, about 3cm in diameter and with a crinkled edge.

Prepare the filling (see page 77), then fill and seal the pasta following the instructions on page 57. If you find it easier, fold the pasta strip over the top of your filling, rather than placing a new sheet on top, as this will help minimize the amount of pasta around the edge. However, you do need to make sure you have enough of a pasta edge to completely seal in the filling.

Tortelli Three Ways

TRE TORTELLI

There is nothing more traditional from Emilia Romagna than spinach and ricotta tortelli. Below, we introduce you to that recipe, but also to two other versions that use nettles (yes, nettles) and parsley. Nettles contain more protein than spinach and the best thing about them is that you can go to your nearest green area and pick them for free. (Just make sure you pick the ones higher up as you don't know where animals have been doing their business.) You can make all three versions and have a 'pick 'n' mix', or choose just one. The recipe for each of these fillings will make more than enough to serve six people, so if you're making all three you will have A LOT – but they're great to freeze. These are all delicious served with Butter and Sage Sauce (see page 92). Or try them with Classic Tomato, Rich Porcini Mushroom or Gorgonzola, Pear and Pancetta Sauce (see page 96, 111 and 105).

Each quantity of filling requires pasta dough made with 400g flour (see page 40) rolled into sheets (see page 48). To assemble and cook the tortelli, see page 57.

SPINACH AND RICOTTA FILLING

Serves: 4–6
Preparation time:
  Pasta: 40 minutes
  Filling: 15 minutes
  Assembling: 1 hour

240g spinach leaves, rinsed and patted dry

250g mascarpone cheese

250g ricotta cheese

100g freshly grated Parmesan cheese, plus extra to taste

fine salt and freshly ground black pepper

freshly grated nutmeg, to taste

1 medium egg, preferably free-range or organic

Steam the spinach in a large covered saucepan, with a little water, for about 5 minutes, until the spinach has wilted. Remove from the heat, drain and leave to cool (you can speed up the cooling process by running cold water over the spinach).

When the spinach is cool enough to handle, squeeze to remove the water. This is a really important step. If there's any excess water in the filling it may cause the pasta to disintegrate, so make sure the spinach is as dry as possible.

Place the cheeses in a bowl and mix in the spinach until well combined. Season, to taste, with salt, pepper, nutmeg and a little extra Parmesan, if you think the mixture needs it. To bind the filling, add the egg and mix well to combine.

NETTLE FILLING

Serves: 4–6
Preparation time:
  Pasta: 40 minutes
  Filling: 15 minutes
  Assembling: 1 hour

240g freshly picked nettles

250g mascarpone cheese

250g ricotta cheese

100g freshly grated Parmesan cheese, plus extra to taste

fine salt and freshly ground black pepper

freshly grated nutmeg, to taste

1 medium egg, preferably free-range or organic

It's a good idea to wear rubber gloves until you've cooked the nettles, to avoid being stung.

Bring a large pan of water to the boil over a medium heat. Submerge the nettles and boil for 5 minutes. They need to be thoroughly cooked through. Remove from the heat, drain and leave to cool (you can speed up the cooling process by running cold water over the nettles).

When the nettles are cool enough to handle, squeeze to remove the water. This is a really important step. If there's any excess water in the filling it may cause the pasta to disintegrate, so make sure the nettles are as dry as possible.

Place the cheeses in a bowl and mix in the nettles until well combined. Season, to taste, with salt, pepper, nutmeg and a little extra Parmesan, if you think the mixture needs it. To bind the filling, add the egg and mix well to combine.

PARSLEY AND LEMON FILLING

Serves: 4–6
Preparation time:
  Pasta: 40 minutes
  Filling: 15 minutes
  Assembling: 1 hour

80g fresh flat-leaf parsley, finely chopped

zest of ½ a lemon

250g mascarpone cheese

250g ricotta cheese

100g freshly grated Parmesan cheese, plus extra to taste

fine salt and freshly ground black pepper

freshly grated nutmeg, to taste

1 medium egg, preferably free-range or organic

In a large bowl, mix together the parsley, lemon zest and the cheeses until well combined. Season, to taste, with salt, pepper, nutmeg and a little extra Parmesan, if you think the mixture needs it. To bind the filling, add the egg and mix well to combine.

Wedding Tortelli with Butternut Squash

TORTELLI PIACENTINI

What makes these tortelli extra special is the way they are folded. Every year when we arrive in Italy we stop off in Bettola, Mum's home town, to eat at our dear friend Rosanna Seghini's restaurant, Le Due Spade. Dad always orders a double portion of their finely folded tortelli. When we were growing up, he often tried to persuade us to spend a month in Italy, learning how to make them. Sadly, we never followed through his dream, until . . . as a thank-you present for their double wedding, Miki and Emi arranged for us all to learn and perfect the method and then had them served at the wedding. This recipe introduces Romina's favourite filling: butternut squash. It's quite sweet but is perfect on an autumn day.

Serves: 6
(makes 50–60 tortelli)

Preparation time:
  Filling: 1 hour
  Pasta: 40 minutes,
  Assembling: 1 hour

Cooking time: 3–5 minutes

pasta dough made with 200g
flour, 2 eggs and a pinch of salt
(see page 40)

flour and polenta, to dust

750g butternut squash, peeled
and cut into 2.5cm chunks

2 tablespoons olive oil

fine salt and freshly ground
black pepper

50g mostarda or ¼ teaspoon
mustard powder

50g amaretti biscuits

25g breadcrumbs

50g freshly grated
Parmesan cheese

freshly grated nutmeg,
to taste

Make your pasta dough and roll it into long sheets (see pages 40 and 48). While it is resting, preheat the oven to 180°C/350°F/ gas 4. Place the butternut squash on a baking tray large enough to accommodate all the pieces in a single layer (you may need to use two trays). Coat with the oil and season with salt and pepper. Roast for 30 to 40 minutes until cooked through. Leave to cool completely.

In a food processor, blend the cooled butternut squash with the mostarda and amaretti biscuits to form a thick paste. Add the breadcrumbs and Parmesan and blend again to incorporate. Season, to taste, with salt, pepper and nutmeg. Transfer the filling to a large piping bag. (If you don't have a piping bag, use a freezer bag with the corner snipped off – see Tips.)

1. On a work surface dusted with flour, cut the pasta sheets into 7.5cm circles using a biscuit cutter or a glass.

2. Starting in the middle of one pasta circle, pipe a triangle of filling about 1.5cm long, ending 0.5cm from the edge.

3. Carefully rest the circle in the palm of one hand with the tallest point of the triangle filling facing you (if you are right-handed, place it in your left hand). With your free hand, fold over the lower sides of the circle to cover the tip of the triangle filling.

4. It will now look like a bouquet of flowers!

5. Working from the side of the circle, alternating sides to create a 'plait', fold and pinch along the centre using your fingers and thumb (but be careful not to press down).

6. When you reach the top, securely fasten the pasta closed by pinching it. Continue in this way, resting each parcel on a tray dusted with polenta.

Bring a large pan of salted water to the boil. Carefully place the tortelli in the boiling water and cook for 3 minutes, until *al dente*. Don't let the water boil too vigorously as this may cause the tortelli to split. Always taste one to check they are cooked before serving.

 TIPS

Don't overfill the piping bag; only fill it halfway. Push the filling to the bottom of the bag and then twist the top to seal. Otherwise, when you squeeze, the filling will come out of the top.

You can make Tortelli Piacentini *with any filling.*

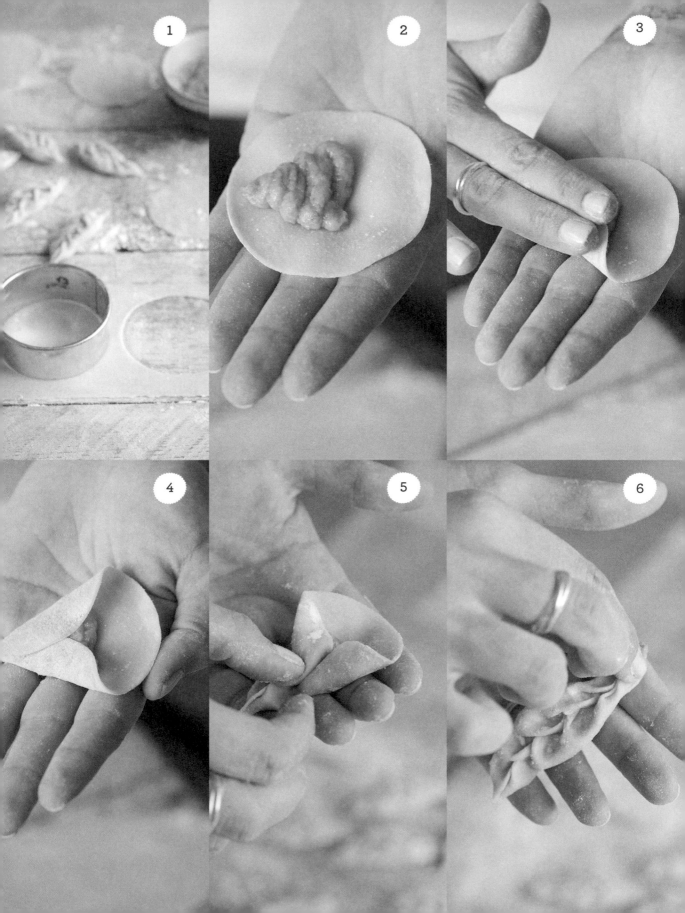

Lobster Ravioli with a Light Butter and Caper Sauce

RAVIOLI ALL'ARAGOSTA

Lobster is very expensive if you serve it on its own but this dish uses just two lobsters to feed six people – a much cheaper way to impress your friends! It's a delicious summer recipe, which can be prepared in advance.

pasta dough made with 300g flour, 3 eggs and a pinch of salt (see page 40)

flour and polenta, to dust

for the filling

2 medium cooked lobsters, to yield 300g meat, chopped into small pieces

20g fresh flat-leaf parsley, finely chopped

½ a red chilli, seeded and finely chopped

zest of a lemon

fine salt and freshly ground black pepper

40g salted butter, melted

for the sauce

10 fresh asparagus spears, woody ends removed, stalks and tips finely chopped

14 cherry tomatoes, finely chopped

20g fresh chives, finely chopped

juice of ½ a lemon

1 garlic clove, peeled and crushed

40g pine nuts, roughly chopped

1½ tablespoons capers, roughly chopped

60g salted butter

extra virgin olive oil, to drizzle

optional: a handful of fennel tops or chopped fresh dill, to garnish

Serves 6 (makes 20–30 large ravioli)
Preparation time:
  Pasta: 40 minutes
  Sauce: 10 minutes
  Filling: 10 minutes
  Assembling: 45 minutes–1 hour
Cooking time: 5 minutes

Make your pasta dough. While it is resting put the asparagus, tomatoes and chives in a bowl with the lemon juice to make the sauce. Using a pestle and mortar, bash the garlic, pine nuts and capers. You want to keep them chunky so don't grind them to a paste. (You can use a food processor for this stage.) Add to the asparagus and tomatoes and mix well to combine. Set aside.

Put the lobster meat in a large bowl with the parsley, chilli, lemon zest and a little salt and pepper. Mix together with the 40g melted butter.

Roll your pasta dough into sheets, then fill and assemble the ravioli with the lobster filling (see page 57).

When you're ready to cook the pasta, bring a large pan of salted water to the boil. Melt the 60g butter in a small saucepan over a medium heat. When it starts to bubble, reduce the heat and stir in the asparagus and tomato sauce. At this point, immediately tip the ravioli into the boiling water, and cook for 2 to 3 minutes, until *al dente*. Don't let the water boil too vigorously as this may cause the ravioli to split. Always taste one to check they are cooked before serving. Using a slotted spoon, transfer the ravioli to serving bowls. Drizzle over 1 or 2 tablespoons of the sauce and a little oil. Garnish with the fennel tops, if using, and serve immediately.

⊗ **TIPS**

To remove the meat from a lobster cooked in its shell, rip off the claws and pull off the tail. Using a sharp knife, slice right down the middle of the tail, pull it open and pull out the meat. Snap the claws in half. Place the flat of your knife across the widest end of each claw and (carefully) bash the top of the blade with a rolling pin until the claw cracks, then pull out the meat.

The lobster filling is also great served in a salad or with our Italian 'Roasties' with Rosemary (see page 204).

Raviolo with an Oozy Egg, Smoked Salmon and Griddled Asparagus

RAVIOLO AL SALMONE AFFUMICATO

We discovered this dish at a Michelin-starred restaurant in Imola, in Emilia Romagna. The head chef there was taught the recipe by his mentor, who cooked this dish for the last king of Italy, Vittorio Emanuele. The recipe is based on a number of different methods and flavours from the region: tortelli, *erbette* filling, ricotta and Parmesan. What we love about this dish is that it mixes one of our favourite recipes, Spinach and Ricotta Tortelli (see page 60), with some very British traditions: poached eggs, smoked salmon and asparagus. See pages 74–75 for step-by-step pictures.

Serves: 4 (makes 4 raviolo)
Preparation time:
  Pasta: 40 minutes
  Filling: 15 minutes
  Assembling: 1 hour

pasta dough made with 200g
flour, 2 eggs and a pinch of salt
(see page 40)

flour and polenta, to dust

20 fresh asparagus spears,
woody ends removed

40g salted butter

freshly grated Parmesan
cheese, to serve

optional: truffle oil, to drizzle

for the filling
125g spinach leaves, washed
and patted dry

50g smoked salmon,
finely chopped

125g ricotta cheese

40g freshly grated
Parmesan cheese

zest of ½ a lemon

fine salt and freshly ground
black pepper

freshly grated nutmeg,
to taste

1 medium egg, plus 4 egg yolks,
preferably free-range
or organic

Make your pasta dough. While it is resting, steam the spinach in a large covered saucepan and cover with a little water and cook for about 5 minutes, until the spinach has wilted. Remove from the heat, drain and leave to cool (you can speed up the cooling process by running cold water over the spinach). When the spinach is cool enough to handle, squeeze to remove the water. This is a really important step. If there's any excess water in the filling it may cause the pasta to disintegrate, so make sure the spinach is as dry as possible, then finely chop it.

In a mixing bowl, combine the spinach and salmon with the ricotta and Parmesan. Season, to taste, with the lemon zest, salt and pepper, and nutmeg. To bind the filling, add the whole egg and mix well. Transfer the filling to a large piping bag (or freezer bag – see page 66).

Roll out 2 pasta sheets (see page 48) and place them on a well-dusted work surface. Pipe 4 rings of filling, about 2.5cm high on one pasta sheet. Carefully place an egg yolk into the centre of each ring and sprinkle with a pinch of salt.

Using your finger, brush a little water around the filling to help the top layer of pasta stick. Carefully lay a rectangle of pasta over the filling, pressing down gently around the outside to remove any air bubbles and seal tightly. Using a 12cm round cutter cut out the ravioli and trim the edges, making sure there are no gaps in the pasta. These ravioli are very delicate so handle them with care. For tips on making ravioli, see page 57. Repeat for the other ravioli.

Cut 4 pieces of baking parchment, each large enough for a ravioli to sit on. Dust with polenta and very carefully transfer the ravioli to the parchment (this will help you move the ravioli when it comes to cooking them).

Heat a griddle over a high heat and cook the asparagus turning occasionally for about 5 minutes, until nicely charred. Remove from the heat.

Bring a large pan of salted water to the boil. Lower the heat so the water is at a gentle rolling boil. Very gently lower each ravioli and baking parchment into the boiling water. The paper will come away from the ravioli in the water. Cook for 3 to 4 minutes. Don't let the water boil too vigorously as this may cause the ravioli to split. Meanwhile, melt the butter in a small pan until it starts to bubble.

Place 5 asparagus stalks on each serving plate. Using a slotted spoon place the ravioli on top of the asparagus. Sprinkle with a little Parmesan and spoon over a tablespoon of the melted butter. Serve, drizzled with a little truffle oil, if desired.

Braised Beef and Parmesan Pasta Parcels in Broth — ANOLINI IN BRODO

Anolini are similar to but much smaller than tortelli – they are more like dumplings. A few weeks before Christmas, all the Chiappa girls get together and spend an entire day rolling, filling and making hundreds of these pasta parcels. We then freeze them to serve as the third course of our six-course Christmas feast. Dad will not have a Christmas lunch without them! This is a local dish from our region of Italy.

Serves: 8–10
Preparation time:
 Filling: 5 hours
 Pasta: 40 minutes
 Assembling: 1 hour
Cooking time: 5 minutes

pasta dough made with 500g flour, 5 eggs and a pinch of salt (see page 40)

flour and polenta, to dust

50g salted butter

1kg lean beef silverside or topside

225g pork tenderloin

1 onion, peeled and sliced

2 garlic cloves, peeled

1 carrot, peeled and chopped

1 stick of celery, sliced

200ml red or white wine

1 tablespoon tomato purée

1 organic beef stock cube

110g breadcrumbs

175g freshly grated Parmesan cheese

3 medium eggs, preferably free-range or organic

fine salt and freshly ground black pepper

¼ teaspoon freshly grated nutmeg

Chicken Broth (see page 218), to serve

Make your pasta dough. While it is resting, melt the butter in a large pan over a medium heat. Cook the beef and pork on all sides for about 5 minutes to seal them.

Add the onion, garlic, carrot, celery and wine and stir gently for 2 minutes. The aim is to burn off the alcohol, leaving just a hint of the lovely wine flavour. Stir in the tomato purée.

Dissolve the stock cube in 300ml boiling water and pour over the meat and vegetables. Place a large piece of baking parchment over the top of the pan and secure it with the lid (the baking parchment will catch any condensation from the underside of the lid so it won't drip onto the meat). Lower the heat and simmer for about 3½ hours, until the meat is tender.

Remove the meat from the pan and transfer to a chopping board. Cover with tin foil and leave to rest. Reserving the cooking liquid, strain and discard the vegetables.

In a small bowl, mix the breadcrumbs with just enough of the cooking liquid to create a paste. Put the meat, the Parmesan, breadcrumb paste and eggs into a food processor, season with salt, pepper and the nutmeg, and blend until smooth.

Roll your pasta dough into sheets and assemble the anolini (see page 58) using the smooth meat mixture as filling.

When you are ready to cook the pasta, bring the chicken broth to the boil over a medium heat. Carefully place the anolini in the broth and cook for 5 minutes, until *al dente*. Always taste one to check they are cooked before serving. Serve the anolini in bowls with a ladleful of the broth and extra grated Parmesan on top.

Traditional Lasagne

LASAGNA TRADIZIONALE

Everyone loves lasagne, and we couldn't write this book without including our recipe. Lasagne often takes the place of a Sunday roast in the Chiappa household – a hearty meal cooked in one dish that can serve a lot of people. Delicious!

Serves: 4–6
Preparation time:
  Basic White Sauce:
  10 minutes
  Pasta: 40 minutes
  Filling: 50 minutes
Assembling: 20–30 minutes
Cooking time: 40 minutes

pasta dough made with 200g flour, 2 eggs and a pinch of salt (see page 40)

50g smoked pancetta, roughly chopped

1 red onion, peeled and finely chopped

1 carrot, peeled and finely chopped

1 stick of celery, finely chopped

1 clove of garlic, peeled and squashed to make a paste

fine salt and freshly ground black pepper

500g good-quality beef mince

½ a wine glass of red wine

2 tablespoons tomato purée

1 x 400g tin good-quality chopped tomatoes

1 organic beef stock cube

1 dried bay leaf

1 x quantity of Basic White Sauce (see page 81)

a splash of milk, if needed

75g freshly grated Parmesan cheese, plus extra to serve

Make your pasta dough and roll and cut it to fit a 30cm x 20cm lasagne dish (see page 48).

Heat a large pan over a medium heat. When hot, lower the heat and fry the pancetta for 2 to 3 minutes, until it starts to crisp up. Stir in the onion, carrot and celery and leave to sweat with the lid on for 10 minutes, until soft and translucent. Sprinkle the garlic with a pinch of salt, mix together, then add to the pan and stir for 1 minute.

Add the beef to the pan, stirring occasionally until browned all over. Pour in the wine and keep stirring for 2 minutes.

Stir in the tomato purée and chopped tomatoes and then add 200ml of boiling water. Crumble in the stock cube, add the bay leaf and stir together. Leave the *ragù* to simmer with the lid on for 15 minutes. Remove the lid and continue to simmer for a further 15 minutes. Taste and season with salt and pepper.

Preheat the oven to 180°C/350°F/gas 4. Bring a large pan of salted water to the boil and blanch the pasta sheets for 30 seconds, until *al dente*. Lay them on a clean tea towel to absorb most of the water. Reheat the white sauce, loosening the sauce with a little milk, if needed.

To assemble the lasagne, start by covering the bottom of the ovenproof dish with a thin layer of white sauce. This will stop the pasta sticking to the base and burning. Add a layer of pasta. Slightly overlap the strips so that there are no gaps, but don't let the pasta curl up the sides of the dish; cut the pieces to fit. Top with a thin layer of white sauce and then a thin layer of *ragù*. Continue until you have 4 or 5 layers of pasta and finish with the white sauce. (Don't use too much *ragù* or white sauce at each stage.)

Sprinkle with the Parmesan and cook in the oven for 30 to 40 minutes until golden brown and bubbling.

Green Lasagne with a Sage and Walnut Pesto

LASAGNA VERDE CON PESTO DI SALVIA E NOCE

Green pasta layered with fresh mozzarella is a vibrant summer twist on our Traditional Lasagne (see page 78). We always have a jar of fresh pesto in the fridge, which makes preparing this dish even easier. You can make this lasagne ahead of time, so if you're hosting a dinner party you'll be free to chat and drink prosecco with your guests while it cooks in the oven.

Serves: 6
Preparation time:
  Basic White Sauce:
  10 minutes
  Pasta: 40 minutes–1 hour
  Pesto: 5 minutes
Assembling: 20–30 minutes
Cooking time: 30 minutes

1 x quantity of green pasta dough (see page 43)

1 x quantity of Basic White Sauce (see opposite)

100g freshly grated Parmesan cheese, plus 40g (optional)

1 x quantity of Sage and Walnut Pesto (see page 118)

300g mozzarella cheese, torn

8 fresh sage leaves

1 teaspoon olive oil

Make your green pasta dough and roll and cut it to fit a 30cm x 20cm lasagne dish (see page 48).

Warm the white sauce over a low heat and stir through the 40g grated Parmesan if you'd like a cheesy sauce.

Preheat the oven to 180°C/350°F/gas 4. Bring a large pan of salted water to the boil and blanch the pasta sheets for 2–3 minutes, to soften slightly. Dip them in cold water and lay them on a clean tea towel to absorb most of the water.

To assemble the lasagne, start by covering the bottom of a 30cm x 20cm ovenproof dish with a thin layer of white sauce. This will stop the pasta sticking to the base and burning. Follow this with a layer of pasta. Slightly overlap the strips so that there are no gaps, but don't let the pasta curl up the sides of the dish; cut the pieces to fit. Spread the pasta with a layer of pesto (about 1½ tablespoons). Follow with a layer of white sauce (about 1½ tablespoons), a layer of mozzarella and a layer of Parmesan. Repeat the layers in this order (pasta, pesto, white sauce, mozzarella, Parmesan) 4 times.

Brush the sage leaves with a little oil and arrange on top. Bake for 20 to 25 minutes, until the top is golden and bubbling gently. Leave to stand for 5 to 10 minutes before serving.

 TIPS

If you don't have time to make fresh pasta, you can use dried lasagne sheets. If you're using dried pasta, make your white sauce a little runnier, as the dish will need extra moisture.

Experiment with different types of pesto. Why not try our Sun-Dried Tomato Pesto (see page 117) with orange pasta (see page 47)?!

BASIC WHITE SAUCE (BÉCHAMEL)
Besciamella

Lots of people worry about making white sauce but you just have to give it a go and be confident. If it doesn't work out the first time, just try again! When we were little and wanted to get involved in the kitchen, this is one of the first things Mum taught us because knowing how to cook besciamella is essential. It is a basic white sauce that appears in many Italian recipes either as part of the recipe – like in lasagne – or as a delicious topping.

Serves: this is the perfect amount for our lasagne recipes (pages 78 and 80)
Cooking time: 10 minutes

80g salted butter
80g plain flour
800ml milk
fine salt and freshly ground black pepper

Melt the butter in a large non-stick saucepan over a medium heat. Whisk in the flour to form a smooth paste. Remove the pan from the heat and slowly add the milk, continuously whisking to incorporate. Taking it off the heat will help you achieve a smooth consistency.

Return to the heat, and whisk until it has formed a thick sauce. Season, to taste, with a little salt and lots of pepper.

Classic Pasta Nests

NIDI CLASSICI

This is another dish handed down from Nonna Luisa, and it is commonly known as *Nidi di Rondine*. It is served at La Locanda Cacciatore, our local restaurant (see page 295), as part of a pasta trio, and when Dad first tasted it, he thought he had died and gone to heaven! '*Nidi*' in Italian translates as 'nests' and you'll see why once you finish this dish.

Serves: 4
Preparation time:
  Basic White Sauce:
  10 minutes
  Pasta: 40 minutes–1 hour
  Filling: 5 minutes
  Assembling: 20–30 minutes
Cooking time: 30 minutes

pasta dough made with 200g flour, 2 eggs and a pinch of salt (see page 40)

1 tablespoon olive oil

300g mushrooms, finely sliced

100ml cognac

fine salt and freshly ground black pepper

1 x quantity of Basic White Sauce (see page 81)

200g thinly sliced Italian ham

75g freshly grated Parmesan cheese

Make your pasta dough and roll it into sheets (see page 48). Preheat the oven to 180°C/350°F/gas 4. Make your white sauce.

Heat the oil in a frying pan over a medium heat and sauté the mushrooms for 4 minutes. Stir in the cognac and cook for 2 minutes. The aim is to burn off the alcohol, leaving just a hint of the lovely cognac flavour. Season, to taste, with salt and pepper.

Cut the pasta sheets into 15cm lengths. Cook 3 or 4 at a time in a large pan of salted boiling water for 2 to 3 minutes, until *al dente*. Overlapping them slightly, lay the cooked pasta sheets on a clean tea towel to create a rectangle of pasta the same size as the tea towel. You will need to move quickly as the pasta will become sticky as it dries.

Leaving a 2.5cm border, spread the pasta with two thirds of the white sauce. Tear the ham and scatter evenly over the white sauce then top with the mushrooms. The filling should be as flat and evenly spread as possible, so it's easier to roll. Sprinkle with the Parmesan.

To roll the *nidi*, position the pasta with a short side facing you. Using the tea towel, gently but firmly roll the pasta over on to itself again and again, keeping it as tight as you can. Finish by rolling it on to a chopping board.

Using a sharp knife, trim the ends and slice into 8 rounds about 2.5cm thick. Place in an ovenproof dish and top with the remaining white sauce. Bake for 20 minutes, until golden and cooked through.

 TIPS

Nidi are great to freeze as individual portions. Bake them from frozen for 30 minutes.

You can use 300g dried lasagne sheets in place of fresh pasta, but make your white sauce a little runnier, as the dish will need extra moisture. It may need to cook a little longer too, so check before serving.

Ricotta, Chilli, Lemon and Grilled Vegetable Nests

NIDI ALLA VERDURA

In our house, traditional *nidi* are made with sheets of pasta, basic white sauce, ham and cooked mushrooms (see page 83), but we've created a summer twist on this classic by using pancakes and fresh vegetables, served with a tomato sauce to cut through the creaminess. The best way to describe this to any Brit is as a savoury Swiss roll . . .

Serves: 4
Preparation time:
  Pancakes: 20 minutes
  Tomato sauce: 20–30 minutes
  Filling and Assembling:
  40 minutes
Cooking time: 30 minutes

1 x quantity of Pancake Batter
(see page 194)

a knob of melted butter

½ quantity of Classic Tomato Sauce
(see page 96)

for the filling
2 red or yellow peppers, quartered
and deseeded

1 small aubergine, cut into 1cm slices

1 small courgette, cut into 1cm slices

olive oil, to drizzle

250g ricotta cheese

a handful of fresh basil leaves,
roughly chopped, plus extra leaves
to garnish

1 large fresh chilli, finely sliced

zest of 1 lemon

fine salt and ground black pepper

85g prosciutto (about 6 slices)

125g buffalo mozzarella

30g freshly grated Parmesan cheese

Make 6 pancakes following the instructions on page 194. Spread out a clean tea towel on your work surface. Lay 3 pancakes next to each other across the top of the tea towel, overlapping them slightly. Brush the edges with a little butter to help them stick together. Make a second overlapping row underneath to create a rough rectangle – make sure there aren't any gaps between the 6 pancakes.

Heat a griddle pan over a high heat and cook the peppers, aubergines and courgettes until charred. Do not use any oil. Remove from the heat, cut into small pieces and drizzle on a little oil. (Alternatively, roast the vegetables in a little olive oil for 30 to 40 minutes, then cut into small pieces.)

Preheat the oven to 180°C/350°F/gas 4. In a bowl, mix together the ricotta, basil, chilli and lemon zest. Season, to taste, with salt and pepper, and mix again.

Leaving a 2.5cm-border, spread a thick layer of the ricotta mixture over the pancakes. Lay the prosciutto on top, then tear the mozzarella into pieces over it. Scatter the vegetables over the mozzarella and sprinkle with two thirds of the Parmesan. The layers should be as even and flat as possible.

To roll the *nidi*, position the pancake rectangle with a short side facing you. Using the tea towel, gently but firmly roll the sheet up as tightly as you can. Finish by rolling it on to a chopping board. Using a sharp knife, trim the ends and slice into 8 rounds about 2.5cm thick. Place in an ovenproof dish, scatter with the remaining Parmesan and drizzle with a little oil. Bake for 10 minutes, until golden and cooked through.

While the *nidi* are cooking, warm the tomato sauce over a low heat. Serve the *nidi* with a generous spoonful of the sauce and a few basil leaves.

Pasta Pie with Potato Filling

TORTA DI PATATE

You may find a pasta pie a little unusual, but don't knock it until you've tried it! It's a regular feature at our annual Italian Picnic – *La Scampagnata* – as it can be made ahead of time and eaten cold (although can be eaten straight out of the oven, and in our house often is!).

Each pie serves: 8–10
Preparation time:
  Pasta: 20 minutes
  Filling: 40 minutes
  Assembling: 15 minutes
Cooking time: 30–40 minutes

for the dough

250g plain flour, plus extra for dusting

2½ tablespoons olive oil

fine salt

100ml warm water

for the filling

1kg potatoes

100g single cream

50g salted butter

freshly grated nutmeg, to taste

1 medium egg, plus 1 egg yolk, preferably free-range or organic

150g freshly grated Parmesan cheese

8 slices of extra-thin pancetta, finely chopped

1 leek, finely sliced

2 sprigs of rosemary, finely chopped

fine salt and ground black pepper

to assemble the pie

olive oil, to grease

1 medium egg, beaten

a few fresh rosemary leaves

Bring a large pan of water to the boil over a high heat. Peel and cut the potatoes into equal-sized pieces, then add to the pan and cook for about 20 minutes, until tender.

While the potatoes are cooking, make the pasta dough. Mix the flour, oil and a pinch of salt in a large bowl or free-standing electric mixer. Slowly add 100ml warm water, mixing gently until it starts to form a paste. Keep mixing until it comes together into a dough then turn out onto a floured work surface. Knead until smooth. You do not need to rest the dough but wrap it in cling film until you're ready, then roll into a long wide sheet of pasta (see page 48). Cut into sheets.

Drain the potatoes leave to dry in the colander for 2 minutes, then return to the pan. Mash until smooth, using a fork or a potato masher. It's important that there aren't any lumps.

Stir in the cream, half the butter and season with nutmeg, to taste. Mix together until well combined and creamy. Mix in the egg and egg yolk. It's important to move quickly so the egg doesn't start to cook in the hot potato. Stir through the Parmesan.

Heat a large pan over a medium heat. When hot, lower the heat and fry the pancetta for 2 minutes, until lightly coloured. Add the leek, rosemary and the rest of the butter and cook for 5 minutes, until the leeks are soft and sweet.

Add the pancetta, leek and rosemary mixture to the mashed potato, season with salt, pepper and more nutmeg, to taste, and mix until well combined.

To assemble the pie, preheat the oven to 200°C/400°F/ gas 6. Lightly grease a 35cm x 25cm rectangular baking tray or a 28cm diameter round tray with a little oil. Ideally the tray should have 3–4cm high sides and a lip around the edge.

Line the base and sides of the tray with sheets of pasta. Lay long sheets side by side and allow them to overlap by 2.5cm to prevent any juices escaping. Aim to leave at least 7.5cm of extra pasta hanging over the edges – this will be used on the pie's top.

Spoon the potato filling into the lined tray. Fold the excess pasta over the top of the filling to create a border. Score the top of the potato with a fork to make a criss-cross pattern.

Brush the top of the pie with beaten egg and scatter with a few lightly oiled rosemary leaves. Cook for 30 to 40 minutes, until the pasta is golden, crunchy and cooked through.

Leave to cool for 15 minutes (this will help the pie keep its shape). Alternatively, leave to cool completely and keep in the fridge to eat the next day.

 TIPS

You can prepare the potato filling and dough the day before and keep them in the fridge. Make sure you bring the dough to room temperature before you roll it out.

This pie is fantastic to freeze once assembled; you can cook it straight from frozen – it will take about 1 hour 15 minutes.

Pasta Pie with Spinach Filling

TORTA DI SPINACI

Like the pasta pie on page 87, this spinach one is also great for making ahead and eating cold (perfect picnic food). It can also be cooked from frozen for 1 hour 15 minutes.

Each pie serves: 8–10
Preparation time:
  Pasta: 20 minutes
  Filling: 5 minutes
  Assembling: 15 minutes
Cooking time: 30–40 minutes

for the dough

250g plain flour, plus extra to dust

2½ tablespoons olive oil

fine salt

100ml warm water

for the filling

470g spinach leaves, washed and patted thoroughly dry

4 tablespoons olive oil

150g freshly grated Parmesan cheese

50g breadcrumbs

fine salt and freshly ground black pepper

freshly grated nutmeg, to taste

to assemble the pie

olive oil, to grease

1 medium egg, beaten, preferably free-range or organic

To make the dough, see page 87. Cut into sheets.

In a large bowl, toss the spinach in the oil until all the leaves are thoroughly coated and glossy. It's much easier if you use your hands for this. Mix in the Parmesan and the breadcrumbs, making sure the leaves are covered. Season, to taste, with salt, pepper and nutmeg, then give everything one final mix.

Preheat the oven to 200°C/400°F/gas 6. Lightly grease a 35cm x 25cm rectangular baking tray or a 28cm diameter round tray with a little oil (ideally use a tray that has high sides and a lip around the edge). Line the base and sides of the tray with strips of pasta. Lay long strips side by side and allow them to overlap by 2.5cm to prevent any juices escaping. Aim to leave at least 7.5cm of extra pasta hanging over the edges – this will be used on the pie's top.

Spoon the spinach filling into the lined tray. It will seem as though there's a lot but it will reduce as it cooks.

Fold the excess pasta over the top of the filling to create a border. (If you like, you can completely cover the spinach pie for a crunchy pasta topping. Patch up any holes with leftover pasta but be careful not to make it too thick.)

Brush the top of the pie with beaten egg. Cook for 30 to 40 minutes, until the pasta is golden, crunchy and cooked through.

Leave to cool for 15 minutes (this will help the pie keep its shape). Alternatively, leave to cool completely and keep in the fridge to eat the next day.

 TIPS

This pie is fantastic to freeze once assembled; you can cook it straight from frozen – it will take about 1 hour 15 minutes.

Speedy Pasta Sauces

A pasta sauce can be one of the quickest things you'll ever make. We're amazed that people buy ready-made pasta sauces when they are so simple to throw together.

LEMON SAUCE
Sugo al Limone

This sixty-second pasta sauce tastes zingy and fresh and immediately lightens any dish. As it's so quick to prepare, make sure your pasta is almost ready before you start the sauce.

Serves: 2–4
Preparation time: 2 minutes
Cooking time: 1 minute

Pasta suggestion: linguine, spaghetti or tortelli

100g salted butter
zest and juice of 1 lemon
fine salt and freshly ground black pepper

Melt the butter in a frying pan over a medium heat. Add the lemon zest and let the butter caramelize – this will take about 1 minute. Squeeze over the lemon juice. Stir in a couple of tablespoons of the pasta cooking water to make the sauce go further, and season to taste.

To serve, either add your cooked, drained pasta to the frying pan and stir to coat, or drizzle over tortelli.

 TIP

For a spicy kick, sprinkle in a teaspoon of chilli flakes when you add the lemon zest.

BUTTER AND SAGE SAUCE
Burro e Salvia

This is a staple sauce served in *trattorie* across northern Italy. It can accompany any type of pasta because it's so simple and light as well as being super-quick to make! We think it goes especially well with Spinach and Ricotta Tortelli (see page 60); the filling has such a rich flavour that it needs a subtle, silky sauce like this.

Serves: 2–4
Preparation time: 30 seconds
Cooking time: 1 minute

Pasta suggestion: works with all pasta types but particularly tortelli

100g salted butter
6–8 fresh sage leaves
fine salt and freshly ground black pepper

Melt the butter with the sage leaves in a frying pan over a medium heat. Cook until the butter turns a light golden colour and the sage leaves start to crisp up. Serve immediately over pasta with salt and pepper, to taste.

 TIPS

Rosemary is another woody herb that works very well with this kind of buttery sauce.

For extra flavour, grate a little Parmesan cheese over the top just before serving.

CREAM, WALNUT AND PARMESAN SAUCE
Sugo alle Noci

A divine combination of cream, cheese and nuts. Like the Butter and Sage Sauce (see opposite), this works well with many types of pasta, as it is full of flavour but we love it with gnocchi. Make sure your pasta or gnocchi are almost ready before you start cooking the sauce.

Serves: 2-4
Preparation time: 5 minutes
Cooking time: 2 minutes

Pasta suggestion: works with all pasta types but particularly gnocchi

300ml single cream

50g walnuts, blitzed in a food processor to a sandy consistency

50g freshly grated Parmesan cheese

fine salt and freshly ground black pepper

freshly grated nutmeg, to taste

Warm the cream in a small saucepan over a low heat (being careful not to boil it). Add the walnuts and Parmesan, and season with salt, pepper and a little nutmeg. Stir until well combined and heat gently until the sauce has thickened. Coat your cooked pasta or gnocchi with the sauce and serve immediately.

 TIP

The longer you leave the sauce on the heat, the thicker it will become, so make it to your liking. If it gets too thick, loosen it with a splash of milk.

OLIVE OIL, GARLIC AND CHILLI
Olio, Aglio e Peperoncino

This is probably one of the easiest and quickest sauces to make. It's one of Michela's favourites, as she often needs to rustle up something speedy after a hectic day – and she's also the family's garlic lover. It's a true classic and sums up Italian cooking at its best: simple, quick and tasty!

Serves: 2-4
Preparation time: 4 minutes
Cooking time: 1 minute

Pasta suggestion: spaghetti or tagliatelle

2 cloves of garlic, peeled and finely sliced

fine salt and freshly ground black pepper

5 tablespoons olive oil

1–2 teaspoons peperoncino powder, cayenne pepper or chilli flakes, depending on how hot you like it

a small bunch of fresh parsley, stalks and leaves separated, finely chopped

freshly grated Parmesan cheese, to serve

Heat the oil in a large frying pan over a medium heat. Fry the peperoncino and parsley stalks for about 45 seconds, until heated through. Season with salt and pepper. Stir in the garlic and cook for 30 seconds; be careful not to let it burn.

Add the drained pasta and stir to coat in the sauce (the pasta doesn't have to be drained completely dry; a little bit of the cooking liquid helps keep the sauce loose). Scatter over the parsley leaves and stir again to combine. Serve with a generous sprinkling of Parmesan.

This little bear is now famous in our hometown, Bardi. Dad remembers paying 100 lire for us each to have a go when we were children.

Classic Tomato Sauce

SUGO AL POMODORO

This is one of the first pasta sauces we learned to cook and it forms the basis of many Italian recipes. Once you master this, you will be able to adapt it to make a different dish every night of the week! This really is the most essential recipe in any Italian kitchen.

It is a very adaptable sauce that you can flavour according to your tastes. As kids we loved mixing in a tin of tuna. Capers, anchovies and olives will turn it into a *puttanesca*, or add some chilli flakes for a fiery *arrabbiata*. Cook with fresh seafood (calamari, prawns and mussels) and you have a really impressive sauce for a dinner party.

Serves: 4
Preparation time: 5 minutes
Cooking time: 20–30 minutes

Dried pasta suggestion: 400g farfalle, penne, spaghetti . . . anything goes!

If making fresh pasta: dough made with 400g flour, 4 eggs and a pinch of salt (see page 40)

1 tablespoon olive oil

1 red onion, peeled and finely chopped

2 cloves of garlic, peeled and crushed

fine salt and freshly ground black pepper

2 x 400g tins good-quality chopped tomatoes

1 tablespoon tomato purée

1 teaspoon caster sugar

¼ teaspoon cayenne pepper

1 organic vegetable stock cube

optional: fresh basil leaves, to serve

Heat the oil in a saucepan over a medium heat and fry the onion for about 4 minutes, until soft and translucent.

Add the garlic to the onion and cook for 30 seconds; be careful not to let it burn. Stir in the tomatoes, tomato purée, sugar, cayenne pepper and stock cube. Simmer for 20 to 30 minutes, until the sauce has thickened.

While the sauce is reducing, cook the pasta in a large pan of salted boiling water until *al dente*. Season the sauce, to taste, with salt and pepper and serve over the cooked pasta, scattered with torn basil leaves.

 TIP

Keep frozen batches of the sauce and when you reheat it, add whatever ingredients you have available: sliced mushrooms, fried bacon, peperoncino powder, pieces of cooked spicy sausage, fresh peppers, olives, mozzarella, spinach leaves . . . Keep it simple, though; Italians don't like complicated food, so only use one or two extra ingredients.

Oozy Tomato Sauce with Spinach and Olives

SUGO AL POMODORO CON OLIVE E SPINACI

This sauce is a simple twist on the Classic Tomato Sauce (see page 96). It has a few extra ingredients that jazz it up if you need to impress in a hurry. The black olives give a wonderful burst of flavour, which contrasts with the creamy mozzarella, and the spinach gives a final explosion of colour. Children will love this oozy tomato sauce with farfalle.

Serves: 4–5
Preparation time: 10 minutes
Cooking time: 20 minutes

Dried pasta suggestion: 400g farfalle, penne or tagliatelle

If making fresh pasta: dough made with 400g flour, 4 eggs and a pinch of salt (see page 40)

½ a red onion, peeled and finely chopped

1 tablespoon olive oil

1 clove of garlic, peeled and crushed

fine salt and freshly ground black pepper

2 x 400g tins good-quality chopped tomatoes

1 tablespoon tomato purée

a pinch of cayenne pepper

1 organic vegetable stock cube

a handful of black olives, stoned

20g freshly grated Parmesan cheese, plus extra to serve

2 x 100g balls buffalo mozzarella

235g baby spinach leaves, washed and patted dry

extra virgin olive oil, to drizzle

Cook the pasta in a large pan of salted boiling water until *al dente*.

Gently fry the onion in the oil over a medium heat for about 4 minutes, until soft and translucent.

Add the garlic to the onion, cook for 1 minute, then add the chopped tomatoes, tomato purée and cayenne pepper, and crumble in the stock cube. Stir everything together and simmer for 5 to 10 minutes, then stir the olives into the sauce and simmer for a further 2 to 3 minutes.

Just before serving, sprinkle the Parmesan over the sauce and stir in torn pieces of the mozzarella. Scatter over the spinach.

Drain the pasta and gently mix it into the sauce. The moisture and heat from the pasta will wilt the spinach. Add a splash of the pasta water to loosen the sauce, if needed. Season to taste with salt and pepper, then serve with a drizzle of extra virgin olive oil and a little extra grated Parmesan on top.

 TIP

Olives should always be bought with their stones still in, as they will be much tastier. We often keep a few spare jars in the cupboard for unexpected visitors (they are great with toasted bread and olive oil as an antipasto). To remove the stones from your olives, squash them with the heel of your hand and the stone will pop out!

Mum's Summer Chilled Tomato Sauce

SUGO DELLA MAMMA

This is Italian-style gazpacho! We used to beg Mum to make this for us when we were on holiday in Italy. It's a chilled tomato sauce served over hot pasta. The hot and cold combination is so delicious on a summer's day and it oozes flavour. There's quite a lot of garlic in it, so be prepared for some strong flavours. It's also great served over fish or meat. And our little cousin Lola loves it!

Serves: 2–3
Preparation time: 5 minutes
Chilling time: 30 minutes
Cooking time: 2 minutes

Dried pasta suggestion:
200g pappardelle

If making fresh pasta:
dough made with 200g flour,
2 eggs and a pinch of salt
(see page 40); silhouette
pasta with herbs (see page 55)

6 large tomatoes
(approx. 600g)

4 cloves of garlic, peeled
and crushed

fine salt and freshly ground
black pepper

a large handful of basil,
roughly chopped

4 tablespoons extra
virgin olive oil

Bring a large pan of water to the boil. Using the tip of a sharp knife, prick the tomatoes all over and cook in the boiling water for 2 minutes, until the skins start to split. Remove from the water and carefully peel off and discard the skins. Roughly chop the flesh then sieve to remove the excess liquid and place in a mixing bowl.

Add the garlic to the bowl with the tomato flesh along with the basil, oil, and season with salt and pepper. Give it a good stir and chill in the fridge for 30 minutes.

When ready to serve, cook the pasta in a large pan of salted boiling water until *al dente*. Place the pasta in a bowl and spoon over the chilled tomato sauce.

 TIP

We love to make this sauce very garlicky but for a less intense flavour use 2 cloves instead of 4.

Bolognese Sauce

RAGÙ

During the filming of our first TV series, *Simply Italian*, we travelled to Bologna to learn how to make authentic Bolognese from expert chef Anna Maria. In this recipe we've combined Anna's tips and tricks with those taught to us by Mum and Nonna Luisa to make the perfect *ragù*. The secret is to let it simmer for 3 hours, so the meat is really tender – and never use tinned tomatoes! Bolognese is a meaty sauce and is not meant to be as tomatoey as most people think. We serve this with wide pappardelle so the meat can cling to the pasta and not slip away like it does with spaghetti.

Serves: 8–10
Preparation time: 15 minutes
Cooking time: 3 hours
15 minutes

Dried pasta suggestion:
800g pappardelle or tagliatelle
– never spaghetti!

If making fresh pasta:
dough made with 800g flour,
8 eggs and a pinch of salt
(see page 40)

100g smoked pancetta, roughly chopped

1 red onion, peeled and finely chopped

1 carrot, peeled and finely chopped

2 sticks celery, finely chopped

1kg good-quality beef mince

a wine glass of red wine

140g tomato purée

2 organic beef stock cubes

2 bay leaves

fine salt and freshly ground black pepper

freshly grated Parmesan cheese, to serve

extra virgin olive oil, to drizzle

Heat a large pan over a medium heat. When hot, lower the heat and fry the pancetta for 2 to 3 minutes, until it starts to crisp up. Stir in the onion, carrot and celery and leave to sweat with the lid on for 10 minutes, or until soft. Add the beef to the pan, stirring occasionally until it has browned all over. Pour in the wine and keep stirring for 2 minutes. The aim is to burn off the alcohol, leaving just a hint of the lovely wine flavour.

Stir in the tomato purée, then add 500ml boiling water. Crumble in the stock cubes, add the bay leaves and stir together. Season with salt and pepper (keep in mind that the Parmesan you will serve it with is quite salty). Leave to simmer with the lid on over a low heat for 3 hours to let the flavours intensify and the beef become tender.

While the sauce is simmering, you could make some fresh pasta (see page 40). When ready to eat, cook the pasta in a large pan of salted boiling water until *al dente*. Drain the pasta, reserving a little of the cooking water.

Place the cooked pasta in a pan over a low heat with 1 or 2 tablespoons of sauce per person – the pasta should not be swimming in Bolognese! Mix together so that the sauce coats the pasta. Add a splash of the cooking water to loosen the sauce, if needed. Finish with a grating of Parmesan and a drizzle of oil. Serve immediately to avoid the pasta overcooking.

 TIP

The ragù *freezes really well, so it's worth making lots of it so you can enjoy it after a hard day at work. You can heat it straight from frozen and it will keep in the freezer for several months.*

Gorgonzola, Pear and Pancetta Sauce

SUGO DI GORGONZOLA CON PERA E PANCETTA

This sauce uses more ingredients than most Italian pasta sauces, which usually combine just three or four basic elements, but we love its salty, sweet and peppery flavours. We serve this with fresh beetroot pappardelle as the mix of colours is fabulous, but it will work well with most types of pasta.

Serves: 2
Preparation time: 15 minutes
Cooking time: 15 minutes

Dried pasta suggestion:
200g pappardelle

If making fresh pasta:
dough made with 200g flour,
2 eggs and a pinch of salt
(see page 40)

6 slices extra-thin pancetta

1 large or 2 small pears, skin on, cored and sliced into 1cm slices

25g salted butter

a few sprigs of fresh flowering or regular thyme, leaves picked

fine salt and freshly ground black pepper

50g chopped walnuts

1 tablespoon brown sugar

100g rocket leaves

75g Gorgonzola, to serve

extra virgin olive oil, to drizzle

Cook the pasta in a large pan of salted boiling water until *al dente*.

Meanwhile, heat a large frying pan over a medium heat. When hot, lower the heat and fry the pancetta for 2 to 3 minutes, until it's nice and crispy. Remove the pancetta from the pan and set aside.

Using the same pan (do not clean it), fry the pear with the butter, thyme and a little salt and pepper for about 3 minutes, until golden. Remove from the pan and set aside.

Place the walnuts in the same pan (you want to keep all the lovely juices from the pancetta and pear) and sprinkle over the sugar. Cook until the sugar has melted, then return the pears to the pan and stir gently to coat them in the caramel. Remove from the heat and leave to one side.

Using tongs, transfer the pasta to the pan with the nuts and pears. Warm through over a low heat while you gently stir in the rocket and crush over half of the pancetta. Give it all a good shake so that the pasta is well coated in the sauce. Serve, scattered with small chunks of Gorgonzola and the remaining pancetta crumbled over the top, and drizzle with a little oil.

 TIP

Instead of slices of pancetta, you could use diced pancetta or even finely chopped bacon, but make sure you get them nice and crispy, as this dish is all about flavour and texture.

Dad's Pasta

PASTA DEL PAPÁ

In true Paola Chiappa style, Mum whipped this up from leftovers in the fridge (and it's a great use of Italian and Welsh ingredients). We had just come back from shopping in Cardiff and were desperately trying to hide from Dad the fact that we'd been out for hours– keeping him happy with food is always the solution! Dad was absolutely bowled over and thought Mum had been slaving away all day to make him something really special. He loved it so much that he always requests it, and so it has now been named *Pasta del Papá*. The secret as to how this pasta sauce came about is out now . . . Love you, Dad!

Serves: 2–3
Preparation time: 5 minutes
Cooking time: 15 minutes

Dried pasta suggestion:
200g tagliatelle or spaghetti

If making fresh pasta:
dough made with 200g flour,
2 eggs and a pinch of salt
(see page 40)

2 tablespoons olive oil

80g pancetta, finely chopped

20g salted butter

1 tablespoon brown sugar

2 small leeks, finely sliced

fine salt and freshly ground black pepper

75g Gorgonzola cheese

Cook the pasta in a large pan of salted boiling water until *al dente*.

Meanwhile, heat the oil in a large pan over a medium heat. When hot, lower the heat and fry the pancetta for 2 to 3 minutes, until it starts to crisp up. Remove the pancetta from the pan and set aside.

Using the same pan (do not clean it), melt the butter and sugar over a medium heat. Add the leeks and cook gently for about 5 minutes, until softened, stirring often and taking care not to burn them. Return the pancetta to the pan with the leeks and turn off the heat.

While the pasta is cooking, add a tablespoon of the pasta water to the sauce and cook over a medium heat for 1 minute. Drain the pasta, then gently stir into the sauce. Season with salt and pepper, crumble over the Gorgonzola and serve immediately.

 TIP

If, like Emi, you are not a fan of Gorgonzola, use another crumbly cheese like goat's cheese or pecorino.

Spaghetti Carbonara

SPAGHETTI ALLA CARBONARA

We've seen so many variations of this classic bacon-and-egg sauce; but we think the simpler the better. The name originally derives from 'carbonaro', the Italian word for 'charcoal burner'. Some people think it was first made to provide a filling meal for Italian charcoal workers, which gives it its nickname 'coal-miner's spaghetti'. Living in the Welsh valleys, we think this is rather appropriate!

Serves: 4
Preparation time: 10 minutes
Cooking time: 10 minutes

Dried pasta suggestion:
400g spaghetti (or use 400g
fresh shop-bought spaghetti)

1 tablespoon olive oil

120g pancetta or bacon, chopped into 1cm pieces

3 medium egg yolks, preferably free-range or organic

200ml single cream

75g freshly grated Parmesan cheese, plus extra to serve

fine salt and freshly ground black pepper

Cook the pasta in a large pan of salted boiling water until *al dente*. About 5 minutes before it's ready, start the sauce.

Heat the oil in a large frying pan over a high heat. When hot, lower the heat and fry the pancetta for 2 to 3 minutes, until it starts to crisp up. Turn off the heat but leave on the stove to keep warm.

Meanwhile, in a small bowl, lightly beat the egg yolks with the cream, Parmesan and a generous amount of black pepper.

Drain the pasta and add to the frying pan with the pancetta. Pour over the egg and cream mixture and stir until well combined. Do not turn the heat back on. The hot pasta will warm the sauce.

Serve with a generous grating of Parmesan and more black pepper.

Rich Porcini Mushroom Sauce

SUGO DI FUNGHI

The richness of this dish comes from the porcini – you'll never get the same flavour from regular mushrooms. Every year in Wales we forage for porcini and it's always a competition to find the best, biggest and largest quantities. We go to great lengths to keep our foraging locations secret! We then slice the porcini and dry them in our airing cupboard to eat throughout the year. One of our earliest memories is of Nonna Luisa's house smelling of drying porcini every autumn.

Serves: 6–8
Preparation time: 15 minutes
Cooking time: 30 minutes

Dried pasta suggestion: works especially with most types of dried pasta but especially great over fresh gnocchi or tortelli (see page 124 or 57)

If using fresh pasta: dough made with 600g flour, 6 eggs and a pinch of salt (see page 40)

20g dried porcini mushrooms

1 clove of garlic, peeled and crushed

fine salt and freshly ground black pepper

2 tablespoons olive oil

1 onion, peeled and finely chopped

3 tablespoons tomato purée

1 organic vegetable stock cube (or mushroom stock cube if available)

optional: 2–3 tablespoons double cream or crème fraîche

In a small bowl, soak the porcini in 600ml boiling water for 10 minutes. Reserving the soaking liquid, drain the porcini and squeeze to remove as much water as possible, then finely chop.

Heat the oil in a heavy-bottomed pan over a medium heat and fry the onion for about 4 minutes, until soft and translucent. Stir in the garlic and cook until it starts to turn golden; be careful not to let it burn. Add the porcini and cook for 1 minute.

Add the tomato purée and stock cube to the porcini water, stir to combine, and then add to the pan. Keep back the last tablespoon or so of the liquid, as the porcini can sometimes be a bit gritty. Reduce the heat and simmer for 20 to 30 minutes, until the sauce has reduced and thickened.

Cook your pasta in a large pan of salted boiling water until *al dente*. Just before serving, season the sauce with salt and pepper and stir through the cream, if using. Drain the pasta, and add to the sauce. Arrange in bowls and serve a little extra sauce over the top – remember that the pasta should be just coated in the sauce, not swimming in a soup.

⊗ TIPS

This sauce freezes very well and can be cooked straight from frozen. Freeze it before you add the cream.

It has quite a meaty texture; for veggies, it works really well as a substitute for the ragú *in our Traditional Lasagne (see page 79–81).*

If you can find them, mushroom stock cubes will make this extra rich and tasty. They are often sold in Italian delis.

Zesty Spring Vegetables

SUGO PRIMAVERA

This is one of Michela's favourite sauces, as it takes just a few minutes to prepare. Plus it's a great feel-good recipe. We always make it in the spring when certain green vegetables are just starting to become available again and it gives us a burst of excitement that summer is on its way! This recipe uses asparagus and fresh peas but you can use any combination of fresh vegetables. The secret is to use a speed peeler so that the veggies are really thin and cook in just a few seconds.

Serves: 2–3
Preparation time: 5 minutes
Cooking time: 5–10 minutes

Dried pasta suggestion:
200g spaghetti, linguine or tagliatelle

If using fresh pasta:
dough made with 200g flour, 2 eggs and a pinch of salt (see page 40)

8–10 fresh asparagus spears, woody ends removed

30g salted butter

1 sprig of fresh rosemary, leaves picked

2 large handfuls peas

zest and juice of 1 lemon

fine salt and freshly ground black pepper

extra virgin olive oil, to drizzle

freshly grated Parmesan cheese, to serve

Cook the pasta in a large pan of boiling salted water until *al dente*. About 5 minutes before it's ready, start the sauce.

Cut off the asparagus tips and keep to one side. Using a speed peeler, peel the stalks into thin strips. (If you don't own a speed peeler, use a potato peeler.)

Meanwhile, melt the butter in a large frying pan. When it starts to bubble, add the rosemary leaves and cook for about 2 minutes, until they start to crisp up. Add the asparagus tips and strips to the frying pan along with the peas and lemon zest. Stir together and season with salt and pepper.

Using tongs, transfer the pasta to the pan and mix to coat in the sauce. Serve with the lemon juice, a drizzle of olive oil and a little grated Parmesan.

 TIP

We sometimes add a tin of tuna along with the vegetables – great if you're feeding hungry men in need of protein.

Fresh Seaside Clam Sauce

SUGO ALLE VONGOLE

When we're in Bardi during the summer, we'll often jump on a train to the crystal-clear blue waters of Liguria's coastline at Cinque Terre. With its network of cliff-top villages, it has breathtaking views of the sea and is one of Italy's hidden gems. This dish transports us back to blissful summer days spent eating fresh seafood. There is an ongoing argument about whether or not it should include tomatoes – we think it should!

Serves: 4
Preparation time: 10 minutes
Cooking time: 10 minutes

Dried pasta suggestion: 400g linguine or tagliatelle

If using fresh pasta: dough made with 400g flour, 4 eggs and a pinch of salt (see page 40)

1kg small clams, scrubbed clean

4 tablespoons olive oil, plus extra to drizzle

4 cloves of garlic, peeled and finely sliced

a large bunch of fresh flat-leaf parsley, leaves and stalks separated, finely chopped

300g cherry tomatoes, halved

fine salt and freshly ground black pepper

200ml white wine

First, sort through your cleaned clams: if there are any that aren't tightly closed, tap them on the work surface and if they still don't close, throw them away.

Bring a large pan of salted water to the boil, ready to cook the pasta.

Heat the oil in a large pan over a medium heat. Add the garlic, parsley stalks and tomatoes, stir together and season with a little salt and pepper. Cook for 3 to 4 minutes, until the tomatoes start to soften – be careful not to burn the garlic.

Cook the pasta in the boiling water until *al dente*. Meanwhile, turn up the heat under the oil, add the clams and white wine, and stir to coat. Cook with the lid on for 3 to 4 minutes, until all the clams have opened, giving the pan a quick shake every so often. If any clams haven't opened, discard them.

Drain and add the pasta to the clams with a handful of the chopped parsley leaves and a generous drizzle of oil. Stir together and serve sprinkled with the rest of the chopped parsley.

Pesto

CLASSIC PESTO
Pesto Classico

Do we really need to say anything about this?! An absolute classic. We usually make ours in bulk and store it in the fridge (with a layer of olive oil on top) or in ice-cube trays in the freezer. Romina loves to spread pesto on toast.

Makes: approx. 250g
Preparation time: 5 minutes

50g fresh basil, leaves picked

2 cloves of garlic, peeled and crushed

50g pine nuts

50g freshly grated Parmesan or pecorino cheese

8 tablespoons extra virgin olive oil, plus extra storing (optional)

fine salt and freshly ground black pepper

Put the basil, garlic, pine nuts, Parmesan and oil in a food processor, and blitz until smooth. Season, to taste, with salt and pepper.

If you're going to store the pesto, transfer it to a sterilized jar (see page 34) and top with olive oil.

 TIP

If you don't have a food processor, crush all the ingredients together in a pestle and mortar and then add the oil.

SUN-DRIED TOMATO PESTO
Pesto di Pomodori Secchi

When tomatoes aren't in season this is a lovely sauce to remind you of summer days. You can stir it through pasta, dollop on top of steamed fish or serve with your Sunday roast! Seal it with a good layer of olive oil and it will keep for months in the fridge.

Makes: approx. 135g
Preparation time: 5 minutes

100g sun-dried tomatoes, in oil

2 tablespoons balsamic vinegar

½ teaspoon salt

½ teaspoon mustard powder

a handful of fresh basil leaves

2 tablespoons extra virgin olive oil, plus extra for storing (optional)

Put all the ingredients in a food processor and blitz until smooth . . . Ta-dah! Add a little more oil if it seems a bit thick.

If you're going to store the pesto, transfer to a sterilized jar (see page 34) and top with olive oil.

 TIP

If you don't have a food processor, finely chop the sun-dried tomatoes, crush all the other ingredients in a pestle and mortar, and add the oil.

SAGE AND WALNUT PESTO

Pesto con Salvia e Noci

This is a fantastic alternative to Classic Pesto (see page 117). The kick of lemon mixed with the walnuts and sage is delicious!

Makes: approx. 295g, enough for the Green Lasagne on page 80
Preparation time: 5 minutes

½ a clove of garlic, peeled

fine sea salt

100g chopped walnuts

zest and juice of 1 lemon

100g freshly grated Parmesan cheese

20 fresh sage leaves

5–8 tablespoons extra virgin olive oil, plus extra for storing (optional)

Pound the garlic with a pinch of salt in a pestle and mortar. Add the walnuts and pound again until they resemble fine breadcrumbs. Tip into a small bowl and stir in the lemon zest and juice, along with the Parmesan.

Bash the sage in the pestle and mortar, grind to a paste and add to the nut mixture. Stir in 5 tablespoons of oil. Keep adding more oil, a little at a time, until it reaches a spreadable consistency. (To speed up this process, you could blitz all the pesto ingredients together in a food processor.)

If you're going to store the pesto, transfer it to a sterilized jar (see page 34) and top with olive oil.

Gnocchi & Risotti

Gnocchi and risottos are two of the easiest dishes to prepare if you follow a few basic tips.

Mum is the Risotto Queen in our family and she loves to make them for us all (partly because they only dirty one saucepan, so there's minimal washing-up!).

People often buy ready-made gnocchi, thinking they are tricky to produce from scratch, but they're simply mashed potato and flour! If you make them yourself, they will also be lighter and fluffier than their shop-bought relatives.

All Italians like to think they're right and we have an ongoing debate in the Chiappa household over whether gnocchi can be considered a pasta dish. *'Pasta'* translates as 'dough' so gnocchi can technically be described as a pasta dish made with a potato 'dough' . . . but some family members disagree – and that's Italians for you.

When we were little, we'd often help Mum make large batches of gnocchi. She'd get us rolling the dough into sausages and cutting them into small pieces using a blunt knife. It was an ideal activity to entertain us on a rainy Welsh day (and there were a lot of these) and we really enjoyed eating something that we had made. Gnocchi are great to freeze and can be cooked straight from frozen in just a few minutes.

In this chapter, we've included classic recipes, as well as a few cheat's risottos that are even quicker and easier to make.

Gnocchi and Risotti Notes

★ When making gnocchi, invest in good potatoes. You might think that any potato will do, but the quality of the potato will make the difference between light and fluffy gnocchi and stodgy or disintegrated failures. Choose a floury potato like King Edward or Maris Piper.

★ An alternative to boiling the potatoes is to bake them in the oven. This helps the potatoes stay dry and gives the gnocchi a more intense flavour. Leave them unpeeled and prick the skin all over. Rub them with a little olive oil and cook for 45 minutes to 1 hour at 180°C/350°F/gas 4, until soft. Peel and continue with the recipe.

★ Gnocchi freeze really well so we often make large batches to save for quick mid-week meals. Put the gnocchi in the freezer, still on their trays, overnight. Once frozen, you can transfer them to freezer bags and they will last for several months. They can be cooked straight from frozen, although they may take a little longer. Always taste one to check they are cooked before serving.

★ Smaller is better. You're more than welcome to cut your gnocchi into any shape and size you like, but we prefer little fingernail-sized gnocchi, as then they're lighter and more delicate – and you can have more on your plate . . .

★ Always use Arborio (or Canaroli) rice for risotto. It has a fat kernel, which absorbs more of the juices from the sauce. Do not attempt a risotto without it!

★ Never overcook the rice. For an Italian, over-cooked rice is worse than overcooked pasta – just don't do it! *Al dente* all the way, and the best way to find out if it's ready is to taste, taste, taste!

★ And on that note: taste, taste, taste! We all cook by taste, not by measurements, so when you're cooking remember to keep tasting. If you think you need a little more salt or pepper or another vital ingredient, just add it. Have a little fun and add whatever you fancy: a splash of wine, a grating of Parmesan, some fresh herbs, a little stock, cream, salt and pepper, or cayenne pepper . . .

★ They don't wait. Both gnocchi and risotto need to be served as soon as they are cooked. Cold gnocchi are not very nice and if you leave your risotto sitting around for too long, it will overcook and turn to mush.

Gnocchi Three Ways with a Creamy Nutty Sauce

GNOCCHI TRICOLORE CON SUGO DI NOCCIOLE

Everyone seems to think that gnocchi are ridiculously difficult to make, but it couldn't be further from the truth – the longest part of the process is cooking the potatoes!

Serves: 4
Preparation time: 1 hour–
1 hour 20 minutes
Cooking time: 6–8 minutes

for the gnocchi

500g floury potatoes (large baking potatoes are best)

fine salt

1–2 medium eggs, preferably free-range or organic

150–200g plain flour, plus extra to dust

2 tablespoons tomato purée

50g rocket leaves, finely chopped

polenta, to dust

for the sauce

300ml single cream

50g hazelnuts, blitzed in a food processor to a sandy consistency

50g freshly grated Parmesan cheese, plus extra to serve

fine salt and freshly ground black pepper

freshly grated nutmeg, to taste

Bring a large pan of salted water to the boil over a high heat. Add the unpeeled potatoes and cook until tender; this could take anywhere from 30 minutes to 1 hour, depending on the size of your potatoes. It's important to cook the potatoes with their skins on, as this helps prevent excess moisture getting in.

Drain the potatoes and peel them while they're still hot – use a tea towel to help hold them. Mash the potatoes while they are still hot, too. Try to make the mash as smooth as possible. Season with salt and leave to cool for 10 minutes.

Add an egg and 150g flour to the mash and mix to form a malleable dough. It needs to be firm and not too sticky. If it seems too soft, add some extra flour; if it's too stiff, add the second egg, yolk first. Taste and add more salt if needed, then divide between three bowls.

Knead the tomato purée into one portion of dough until it's evenly distributed. Add the rocket to another batch and knead until well mixed through. Leave the final batch plain. If, at any point, the batches of dough seem too moist, add a little more flour.

Dust the work surface with flour. Roll each ball of dough into a long sausage shape – the narrower the better. Using a blunt knife, work your way along the dough cutting it into small, evenly sized squares, about 1cm wide. Place your finished gnocchi on trays dusted with polenta. Be careful not to overcrowd the trays. (At this point you can freeze the gnocchi.)

Bring a large pan of salted water to the boil and prepare your sauce. Pour the cream into a small saucepan and place over a low heat. Add the hazelnuts and Parmesan, and season with salt, pepper and nutmeg. Stir well and heat gently until the sauce thickens.

Carefully place the gnocchi in the boiling water and cook for about 2 minutes, until they start floating to the top. Always taste one to check they are cooked before serving. Using a slotted spoon, transfer the gnocchi to a serving dish. Pour over the creamy sauce and finish with a little extra Parmesan.

Baked Gnocchi from Lugano

GNOCCHI ALLA ROMANA (OR, AS WE CALL IT, GNOCCHI DI LUGANO)

This is not what most people think of as a 'traditional' gnocchi as the preparation is very different. However, it's a very versatile recipe that Mum brought back from Lugano, on the Swiss–Italian border, where she worked as an *au pair*. It is a favourite with children as it can be cut into different shapes – we used to use biscuit cutters to make stars! Traditionally, this dish is made using semolina but we have adapted it so we can use instant polenta. It's an incredibly versatile recipe and can be served as a starter, main course or side dish.

Serves: 6–8 as a starter or side dish, 4 as a main course
Preparation time: 20 minutes
Chilling time: 30 minutes
Cooking time: 20 minutes

1 litre milk

fine salt and freshly ground black pepper

300g instant polenta or semolina

2 medium egg yolks, beaten, preferably free-range or organic

100g salted butter

150g freshly grated Parmesan cheese

Preheat the oven to 200°C/400°F/gas 6.

In a heavy-bottomed pan, bring the milk almost to the boil over a medium heat. Season with salt and pepper. Slowly pour in the polenta, whisking for about 3 minutes, until you have a smooth, thick mixture. Remove from the heat and add the egg yolks, half the butter and half the Parmesan. Mix together thoroughly.

'Grease' a large baking tray (about 35cm x 25cm) with a little water, then tip the polenta into the tray. Press the mixture flat with the palms of your hands or a spoon to a thickness of 1.5cm. Leave to cool in the fridge for 30 minutes.

When completely cool and set, turn out the polenta onto a flat surface and cut out circles with a biscuit cutter or a glass. Lay the pieces in an overlapping layer on the bottom of an ovenproof dish. Dot the polenta with the remaining butter, sprinkle with the rest of the cheese and bake for 15 to 20 minutes, until golden brown with a light crust.

 TIPS

Instead of dotting with butter before cooking, try scattering with small pieces of Gorgonzola.

For a more substantial meal, top with goat's cheese, crispy bacon and crumbled walnuts before baking.

BAR CENTRALE

Pane · Pasta · Dolci

FRUTTA VERDURA

ROSTICCERIA Fiorentini

MACELLERIA

GASTRONOMIA

 MACELLERIA EQUINA

Risotto from Parma

RISOTTO ALLA PARMIGIANA

This simple risotto is served in restaurants throughout Italy and it forms the base for hundreds of delicious variations. This was one of our favourite meals as kids because we loved Parmesan cheese and we would always gobble it up. Little did we know that this was what Mum cooked when she hadn't been food shopping.

Serves: 4
Preparation time: 10 minutes
Cooking time: 30 minutes

30g salted butter

1 tablespoon olive oil

1 onion, peeled and finely chopped

350g Arborio rice

a wine glass of white wine (optional, but good)

900ml hot organic vegetable stock

100g freshly grated Parmesan cheese

fine salt and freshly ground black pepper

optional: 2 tablespoons cream cheese, crème fraîche or fresh cream, to serve

Melt the butter with the oil in a heavy-bottomed pan (large enough to hold about 2 litres of water) over a medium heat. Fry the onion for about 5 minutes, until lightly golden.

Stir in the rice and let it absorb the oil. Keep stirring so the rice doesn't stick to the pan and it gets coated in the oil. Pour in the wine, if using, and continue to stir for about 2 minutes. The aim is to burn off the alcohol, leaving just a hint of the lovely wine flavour.

Add the hot stock to the rice, one ladleful at a time. Stir between each addition until the liquid is almost completely absorbed before adding the next ladleful. Continue until you've added all the stock, stirring continuously. This will take about 20 minutes. To check the rice is cooked, taste a few grains; it should be soft but with a slight bite. If it needs a bit longer, add a little hot water.

Stir in the Parmesan, season with salt and pepper and stir in the cream cheese, crème fraîche or fresh cream if using.

 TIPS

Dad loves to add a 400g tin of chopped tomatoes after stirring in the rice and to substitute the white wine for red.

Experiment with any veggies you have to hand. Dice them small and add them after you've stirred in the rice.

Risotto with Asparagus

RISOTTO AGLI ASPARAGI

The wonderful thing about risotto is that you only use one pan, so you don't have loads of washing up. This is one of Dad's all-time favourite risottos, and Mum used to make it for us when we were little as it's a great way to get kids to eat some greens.

Serves: 4
Preparation time: 10 minutes
Cooking time: 30 minutes

30g salted butter

1 tablespoon olive oil

1 onion, peeled and finely chopped

350g Arborio rice

a wine glass of white wine (optional, but good)

1 x 250g tin asparagus, drained and roughly chopped

10 fresh asparagus spears, woody ends removed, stalks chopped, tips left whole

900ml hot organic vegetable stock

100g freshly grated Parmesan cheese

fine salt and freshly ground black pepper

optional: 2 tablespoons cream cheese, crème fraîche or fresh cream, to serve

Melt the butter with the oil in a heavy-bottomed pan (large enough to hold about 2 litres of water) over a medium heat. Fry the onion for about 5 minutes, until lightly golden.

Stir in the rice and let it absorb the oil. Keep stirring so the rice doesn't stick to the pan. Pour in the wine, if using, and continue to stir for about 2 minutes. The aim is to burn off the alcohol, leaving just a hint of the lovely wine flavour. Add the tinned and fresh asparagus and stir in gently.

Add the hot stock to the rice, one ladleful at a time. Stir between each addition until the liquid is almost completely absorbed before adding the next ladleful. Continue until you've added all the stock, stirring continuously. This will take about 20 minutes. To check the rice is cooked, taste a few grains; it should be soft but with a slight bite. If it needs a bit longer, add a little hot water.

Stir in the Parmesan, season with salt and pepper, then stir in the cream cheese, crème fraîche or fresh cream if using.

 TIP

Asparagus has quite a mild flavour so you could substitute the cream cheese with a stronger cheese – Miki likes to use goat's cheese, and Dad prefers Gorgonzola.

Cheat's Risotto with Courgette, Ham and Cheese

RISOTTO CON ZUCCHINI, FORMAGGIO E PROSCIUTTO COTTO

When Emi was a nanny for a family in Lugano, she would often cook this quick risotto for the children. They loved the combination of soft cheese and ham . . . and didn't guess that there were vegetables hidden in there.

Serves: 2–3
Preparation time: 10 minutes
Cooking time: 15 minutes

1 courgette

250g Arborio rice

110g Italian cooked ham

3 tablespoons cream cheese

30g freshly grated Parmesan cheese, plus extra to serve

fine salt and freshly ground black pepper

Grate the courgette using the wide teeth on a cheese grater.

Put the rice and courgette into a large pan of salted water and cook for 15 minutes (there's no need to wait for the water to boil before adding the rice and courgette). To check the rice is cooked, taste a few grains; it should be soft but with a slight bite.

Meanwhile, chop the ham into small pieces.

Drain the rice and courgette and return to the hot saucepan. Stir in the cream cheese, Parmesan and ham. Mix well to combine and season, to taste, with salt and pepper. Serve immediately, topped with extra grated Parmesan.

 TIPS

To add extra flavour, replace the salted water with chicken stock.

We often stir through three Bel Paese soft cheeses instead of using cream cheese. You can find these in Italian delis.

Cheat's Mushroom Risotto

RISOTTO AI FUNGI

Mum is Queen Risotto-Maker and Dad often tells her that she should open a risotto restaurant. This recipe is from a good friend, Franca, from Camaiore, and if you want a quick, foolproof risotto it is the one for you . . .

Serves: 4
Preparation time: 15 minutes
Cooking time: 15 minutes

350g Arborio rice

20g dried porcini mushrooms

1 small onion, peeled and finely chopped

1 tablespoon olive oil

1 organic vegetable stock cube

optional: ¼ teaspoon peperoncino powder or cayenne pepper

80g freshly grated Parmesan cheese

1 tablespoon cream cheese, crème fraîche or fresh cream

fine salt and freshly ground black pepper

Put the rice into a large pan of salted water and cook for 15 minutes (there's no need to wait for the water to boil before adding the rice). To check the rice is cooked, taste a few grains; it should be soft but with a slight bite.

Meanwhile, in a small bowl, soak the porcini in 400ml boiling water for 10 minutes. In a frying pan, gently fry the onion in the oil for about 4 minutes, until soft and translucent. Remove from the heat.

Reserving the soaking liquid, drain the porcini and roughly chop. Add the crumbled stock cube, mushrooms and peperoncino, if using, to the onions. Stir in the porcini soaking liquid, keeping back the last couple of spoonfuls, as it may be a bit gritty.

Drain the rice and return to the hot pan. Add the mushroom sauce to the rice, mixing to combine. Stir in the Parmesan and cream cheese, crème fraîche or fresh cream and season, to taste, with salt and pepper.

⊗ TIPS

A mushroom stock cube stirred into the porcini water will make this extra tasty. You can buy them in most Italian delis.

You can replace the porcini with 200g fresh mushrooms. You won't need to soak these; slice them and fry with the onion. The sauce won't have such a strong flavour, so you'll need to add more seasoning or use a mushroom stock cube (see above).

The mushroom sauce can be made in advance, so all you need to do is boil the rice when you're ready to eat. It will keep in the fridge for a few days or you can freeze it for several months.

Seafood Risotto

RISOTTO AI FRUTTI DI MARE

You'll find a version of *Risotto ai Frutti di Mare* at most Italian seaside resorts. It's Michela's favourite summer beach food and she eats it every time we hit the shore on our Italian holidays. Cooking with seafood is really simple once you get the hang of it – ask your friendly fishmonger if you need any advice.

Serves: 4
Preparation time: 20 minutes
Cooking time: 30 minutes

2 tablespoons olive oil

2 small fresh chillies, deseeded and finely chopped

2 cloves of garlic, peeled and finely chopped

8 baby squid, prepared, cleaned and sliced into 1cm rings

350g Arborio rice

a wine glass of white wine

900ml hot fish stock

100g cockles or shelled mussels

200g raw prawns, shelled (if frozen, make sure they're fully defrosted)

8 raw king prawns, heads and tails left on (if frozen, make sure they're fully defrosted)

fine salt and freshly ground black pepper

optional: a handful of fresh flat-leaf parsley, picked leaves

In a heavy-bottomed pan (large enough to hold about 2 litres of water) heat 1 tablespoon of oil over a medium heat. Add half the chilli, half the garlic and all of the squid. Cook for about 2 minutes, until the squid is just cooked through. Be careful not to burn the garlic.

Stir in the rice and let it absorb the oil. Keep stirring so the rice doesn't stick to the pan. Pour in the wine and continue to stir for about 2 minutes. The aim is to burn off the alcohol, leaving just a hint of the lovely wine flavour.

Add the hot stock to the rice, one ladleful at a time. Stir between each addition until the liquid is almost completely absorbed before adding the next. Continue until you've added all the stock, stirring continuously. This will take about 20 minutes. Add the cockles or mussels and cook for 5 minutes before adding the shelled prawns.

Meanwhile, in a separate pan, heat the remaining 1 tablespoon of oil. Fry the king prawns with the remaining chilli and garlic for 2 minutes, until they are nicely pink and cooked through.

To check the rice is cooked, taste a few grains; it should be soft but with a slight bite. If it needs a bit longer, add a little hot water. Season, to taste, with salt and pepper. Remove from the heat and serve in bowls, with the king prawns arranged on top and sprinkled with the parsley leaves, if using.

 TIP

Try experimenting with different fish. Emi likes to make this with just prawns and Miki likes to use mussels or clams still in their shells, so she can get her hands in the dish! If you're nervous about cooking with seafood, you can buy a seafood mix from the supermarket. Stir it all in when you would be adding the cockles – the seafood will only take a few minutes but make sure it's cooked through before serving.

Pizza & Dough

Ahhh, pizzas and doughy treats! A homemade thin-crust pizza has to be one of the healthiest meals you can eat. We're always amazed that people think pizzas are bad for you . . . Obviously, if you eat a processed, deep-pan pizza from a fast-food chain or supermarket, then, yes, it will be full of salt, fat and other nasties. But making one in your own home can be a delicious, filling and healthy treat – simply flour, water, mozzarella, tomatoes and a little olive oil. *Tutto qui!*

We've also included some of our favourite recipes that use the same basic ingredients as pizza dough – try the Chisurin on page 150. It's a seriously good but naughty way to use up leftover dough!

The Chiappas are well known for our Pizza Sundays, when all the family get together around the pizza oven in the garden – but we make the same meal in our kitchen oven during the winter months when it's a bit too cold and wet to head outdoors. As always, it's a family affair: Mum usually makes a big batch of dough, us girls prepare the toppings, and Dad and Uncle Laz argue over who prepares the fire.

Our basic recipe on page 145 provides simple tips for preparing a pizza in your kitchen oven, but for those of you who are considering an outdoor pizza oven, here are a few extra words of wisdom.

* You don't need anything too fancy for a pizza oven, but you must invest in a stone pizza shell. This is a dome-like structure, which can heat to a high temperature.

* You need your oven to be HOT! Dad will often light the oven early in the morning (or even the day before if it hasn't been used all winter) and you need to keep feeding it with wood to heat the stone properly.

* Once the oven is hot enough and the wood has burned down, push the embers to the side or back of the oven with a pizza paddle. Make sure you bang the paddle against the stone to remove any excess ash.

* A good pizza paddle makes the whole process a lot simpler and you can use it to slide your pizza into and out of the oven. Make sure you dust it with flour so that the pizza doesn't stick.

* If your oven is at the right temperature, the pizzas should cook in less than 2 minutes – great for a production line or when you have hungry children waiting!

* If the stone cools down, push the hot embers back over the centre of the stone for a few minutes, and then push them to one side to begin cooking again.

Chiappa Family Pizzas

PIZZE DELLA FAMIGLIA CHIAPPA

This recipe is super-simple and works really well with an outdoor pizza oven or a regular kitchen oven. Miki's favourite toppings are mushroom and onion; Emi likes mascarpone, sliced cherry tomatoes and rocket; and Romina prefers ham and sweet chilli peppers.

Serves: 4
Preparation time: 30 minutes
Resting time: 30 minutes–1 hour
Cooking time: 15 minutes

for the dough

7g quick-acting yeast or 30g fresh yeast

1 tablespoon caster sugar

500g Tipo '00' flour, plus extra to dust

1 teaspoon fine salt

2 tablespoons olive oil, plus extra to grease

for the topping

1 x 400g tin good-quality plum tomatoes

1 tablespoon olive oil

1 tablespoon dried oregano, plus extra to serve

1 teaspoon fine salt

½ teaspoon peperoncino or cayenne pepper

200g freshly grated mozzarella cheese

plus toppings of your choice – it's important not to overload the pizzas, so stick to a maximum of 3 toppings per pizza

To make the dough, dissolve the yeast and sugar in 250ml warm water and allow to rest for 5 to 10 minutes. (The yeast should make the water froth and bubble, but don't worry if it doesn't happen.)

Mix the flour and salt together in a bowl. Using a fork, mix in the yeasty water until it starts to form a dough. Add the oil and bring together into a smooth dough.

Turn the dough onto a floured surface and knead until it has an elastic, smooth texture – time to give your arms a workout! If the dough sticks to your hands, add a little extra flour. Place the dough back into the bowl and cover with a damp tea towel. Leave in a warm spot for 30 minutes to 1 hour, until it has doubled in size. Meanwhile, preheat the oven to its maximum temperature, 250°C/480°F/gas 9.

In a food processor, blend the tomatoes with the oil, oregano, salt and cayenne pepper. Get the mozzarella and your choice of toppings ready and grease 4 baking trays (approximately 35cm x 25cm) with a little oil.

When your dough is ready, divide into 4 tennis-ball-sized amounts and mould until smooth. (If not using immediately, cover with cling film or a damp tea towel for up to 2 hours.) On a floured surface, roll each of the balls of dough to fit the baking trays. The dough should be quite thin – about the thickness of cardboard. Transfer the pizza bases to the trays.

Place a ladleful of the tomato sauce in the centre of each base and spread towards the edges, leaving a 1cm edge for the crust to form. Sprinkle each pizza with grated mozzarella and your choice of toppings.

Place in the hot oven and cook for 10 to 15 minutes until the base is cooked and golden. Serve, sprinkled with a little oregano.

Focaccia College House

When Michela and Dan opened The College House in Cardiff in 2009, Dan spent several weeks in Italy with our cousin and expert baker, Paolo Chiappa. Focaccia takes time to prepare, as the dough needs plenty of time to rise and a lot of elbow grease – but it's worth the effort!

Makes: 1 x 500g focaccia
Preparation time: 45 minutes
Resting time: 2 hours
Cooking time: 20 minutes

12g fresh yeast or
4g quick-acting yeast

½ teaspoon caster suagr

500g Tipo '00' flour, plus
extra to dust

1 teaspoon fine salt

1 teaspoon brown sugar

50ml olive oil, plus
2 tablespoons

100ml water mixed with
2 teaspoons fine salt

To make the dough, dissolve the yeast and caster sugar in 300ml warm water.

Mix the flour, salt and brown sugar together in a large bowl. Mix in the yeasty water until it starts to form a dough. Add the 50ml oil and bring together to form a smooth dough.

Turn the dough onto a floured surface and knead until it has an elastic, smooth texture. If the dough sticks to your hands, add a little extra flour. Place the dough back in the bowl and cover with a damp tea towel. Leave in a warm place for 1 hour, until the dough has doubled in size. Remove the dough from the bowl, knock out the air and knead again. Put back in the bowl, cover with the cling film and leave to one side for 5 minutes.

Grease a high-sided 33cm x 25cm baking tray with 1 tablespoon of oil. Place the dough on the tray, gently flattening and spreading with your hands. Cover with the tea towel and leave for 20 minutes.

Flip the dough over and stretch it out towards the edges of the tray with your fingertips and palms. Use your fingertips to create deep impressions on the surface of the dough. Cover with cling film and leave for 30 minutes. Meanwhile, preheat the oven to its maximum temperature, 250°C/480°F/gas 9.

Pour the rest of the oil and the salted water over the dough so that it runs into and fills the holes. Bake in the oven for 10 to 15 minutes, until the top of the focaccia is golden brown. Turn down the heat to 180°C/350°F/gas 4 and cook for a further 5 minutes, until cooked through.

 TIP

We like to toss a finely sliced white onion or a handful of cherry tomatoes in olive oil and salt and spread over the focaccia before baking. Then scatter with rocket (see photograph on opposite page) or chopped olives before serving.

Nonno's Mini Sausage Rolls

SALSICCIE IN CAMICIA

Our Nonno Muk-a-Muk (as we call him!) owned a little bakery in Bridgend, South Wales, and we would often spend weekends baking with him. His kitchen was always filled with clouds of flour. Sausage rolls were his speciality and he loved using delicious Italian sausages, which remind us of summer nights in Italy when we used to barbecue at our local river under the stars. They are coarse meaty sausages, rustic and juicy.

Makes: 24 sausage rolls
Preparation time: 10 minutes
Cooking time: 20 minutes

plain flour, to dust

375g pack of ready-rolled puff pastry

400g good-quality Italian sausages

2 sprigs of fresh rosemary, finely chopped

30g breadcrumbs

fine salt and freshly ground black pepper

1 medium egg, preferably free-range or organic

Preheat your oven to 200°C/400°F/gas 6.

On a well-floured work surface, roll out the pastry into a rectangle about 70cm x 40cm. It should be quite thin – about the thickness of cardboard. Cut lengthways into 4 even strips.

Slice the sausages lengthways, peel off their skins and discard. Break the meat into a bowl. Add the rosemary and breadcrumbs (the breadcrumbs will absorb the fat in the sausages when they cook so the pastry won't become soggy). Season with salt and lots of pepper. Using your hands, mix together until well combined.

Divide the sausage mixture into 4. Roll each portion into a long sausage shape the same length as the pastry strips and about 2cm wide.

Beat the egg and brush it along each of the pastry strips. Place the sausage filling on the pastry strips. Fold over one edge of the pastry to meet the other and seal by pressing the edges together with a fork. Brush more egg wash over the top of the pastry.

With a sharp knife, cut the rolls into 2.5cm lengths and place on a baking tray lined with baking parchment.

Bake in the oven for 20 minutes, or until golden and the pastry has puffed up. Cool on a wire rack.

⊗ TIPS

We like to double up the quantity and keep some uncooked sausage rolls in the freezer. That way you have spares for unexpected visitors You can cook them from frozen; just make sure they are properly cooked all the way through.

For an extra twist, try adding a little lemon zest or a diced apple to your sausage meat.

Fried Dough

CHISURIN / PASTA FRITTA

These are a real guilty pleasure and we make them whenever we have leftover pizza dough. Quite simply, they're deep-fried dough parcels filled with cheese, which becomes deliciously oozy when melted. It's another recipe we do when all the family are together. We usually get the men chopping the cheese, while the girls get their elbows busy rolling out the dough. There are so many different names for this dish across Italy. In our Mum's town, Bettola, they call it *bortelina*, whereas in Pilati it's *chisurin*.

Serves: Depends how many you eat! Makes 18-20
Preparation time: 10 minutes
Cooking time: 5 minutes

½ quantity of pizza dough (see page 145)

plain flour, to dust

600g caciotta cheese (or a block of Taleggio or Cheddar cheese), chopped into 0.5cm cubes

vegetable oil, for frying

fine sea salt

Roll the dough onto a well-floured work surface. The dough should be quite thin – about the thickness of cardboard.

Cut the dough into rough rectangles, about 10cm x 5cm. Place a cube of cheese in one half and fold the dough over to create a square parcel. Press around the edges to seal – this is important to stop the cheese from escaping.

Pour the oil into a pan to a depth of 2cm and place over a medium heat. Heat the oil until a small piece of the dough dropped in bubbles quickly turns golden brown. Fry the pieces of dough, a few at a time, for 3 to 4 minutes, turning to cook on both sides, until golden and crispy. Take care not to burn them.

Use a slotted spoon to remove the parcels from the oil and drain on kitchen paper. Serve immediately, sprinkled with salt. Repeat with the rest of the dough parcels (you may need to add more oil as you go along).

 TIP

Lots of trattorie *prepare this fried dough without the cheese and serve it as an* antipasto *with a selection of cured meats.*

Melted Cheese in a Pan

FORMAGGIO NEL PADELLINO

Whilst most households might eat cheese on toast or a boiled egg on a Sunday evening, us Chiappa girls are usually huddled around a saucepan with our Dad. *'Formaggio nel Padellino'* literally means 'cheese in a pan' but whenever Dad suggests having this dish, we all get excited, as if he has just announced a Christmas feast. It fills us with memories of dark winter evenings, coming in from the cold and clustering around a pan for some hot, gooey cheese and bread. The bottom layer of cheese goes crispy and crunchy and it's always a fight to get those tasty final bits!

Serves: As many as can fit around the pan!
Preparation time: 1 minute
Cooking time: 2 minutes

400g caciotta cheese (or Cheddar or Taleggio cheese)

crusts of bread or toast

Cut the cheese into 0.5cm slices and melt in a non-stick frying pan over a medium heat. Once the cheese has melted, remove from the heat and immediately start dunking your bread in the delicious oozy goodness. Don't forget to peel the crusty base off the bottom of the pan – this is the really tasty part that we all squabble over!

 TIP

We sometimes add some capers or chopped olives to the melted cheese for extra flavour.

Mains

In Italy, the first course (*primo piatto*) is usually vegetarian and pasta based. However, meat or fish is the hero of the second course (*secondo*), which we serve accompanied by a selection of sides (*contorni*).

Our Nonno Pino is from a village right up in the Apennine Mountains, where the hunting season provides an important livelihood for many. Come the autumn, game such as wild boar, pheasant and hare can be found in abundance in the local trattorias. So much so, that when we arrive back in the village in the summer, many of our aunts and friends will drop packets of frozen meat on our doorstep to help spread their supplies from the previous year – and Mum will immediately start to look panicked. She will have been looking forward to fresh salads and quick-and-easy cooking for our holiday, not slaving over a joint of meat or hotpot! You have to love the extended family.

Regional and seasonal meats are celebrated in the local *feste*, too. Each summer our local town, Bardi, hosts the *Festa dell'Emigrante* (the Emigrants' Festival). Local meats and sausages are served either as a pasta dish or with hot polenta, and we eat at wooden trestle tables and enjoy the local music and good wine. In Santa Giustina, a little village nearby, they cook wild boar in a large fire pit in the ground. Locals dig a one-metre-square pit in a field and spend days feeding the fire. Once the right temperature has been reached, the embers are allowed to die down and the hog is put into the hole and covered up. The heat from the ground creates one of the best slow roasts you can imagine. Again, this is fully celebrated with lots of wine!

In this chapter, we have included some of our family's favourite dishes. We particularly love the winter warmers, such as Mum's Braised Beef in Red Wine Stew, which is great for feeding a crowd (see page 183), or the Hunters' Hotpot or Nonna's Hearty Sausage Stew (see page 173 or 186), both of which can be cooked in one pot – unfussy, stress-free, oven-to-table food!

Ma's Meatballs

POLPETTE DELLA MAMMA

MAMMA'S MEATBALLS! Come on, we know you're all rolling your eyes at such a stereo-typical dish. Well, they are flipping good, so we couldn't leave them out. You can serve these with Italian 'Roasties' (see page 204), but we love to mix them into the Classic Tomato Sauce (see page 96) and serve with creamy polenta.

Serves: 4–5
Preparation time: 5 minutes
Cooking time: 10 minutes

500g Italian sausage meat

100g freshly grated
Parmesan cheese

1 clove of garlic, peeled
and finely chopped

100g breadcrumbs

2 medium eggs, preferably
free-range or organic

optional: ½ a teaspoon of
ground fennel seeds

a small handful of chopped
fresh parsley

1 teaspoon fine salt

½ teaspoon freshly ground
black pepper

1 tablespoon olive oil

Put all the ingredients apart from the oil into a large bowl and mix together with your hands. Shape into walnut-sized balls.

Heat the oil in a frying pan over a medium heat and cook the meatballs for about 10 minutes, turning regularly until browned all over and cooked through.

 TIPS

Mix in half a teaspoon of chilli powder for some heat.

Italian sausage meat often has fennel pollen in it. If using regular sausage meat, ground fennel seeds will mimic the taste.

For a healthier option, you can bake the meatballs in the oven at 180°C for about 30 minutes until golden brown and cooked through.

Fillet Steak Wrapped in Pancetta and Rosemary

FILETTO DELLO CHEF

Emi's husband likes to eat meat at every meal and so, with the addition of pancetta and rosemary, his favourite steak has been given an Italian twist. If you double up the quantities, it works well for a dinner party, too.

Serves: 2
Preparation time: 2 minutes
Cooking time: 4–14 minutes, depending on how you like your steak cooked

2 fillet steaks, 2.5cm thick

fine salt and freshly ground black pepper

4 extra-thin slices of pancetta

2 sprigs of fresh rosemary

2 tablespoons olive oil

a wine glass of red wine

Season the steak well with salt and pepper. Wrap 2 slices of pancetta around the sides of each steak.

With a sharp knife, make a slit through the centre of each steak and push through a sprig of rosemary.

Heat the oil in a frying pan over a high heat. When hot, fry the steak for 2 minutes on each side for rare, 4 minutes for medium, and 6–7 minutes for well done.

When your steak has been cooked to your liking, pour the wine over the steak, heat it through for 30 seconds and serve immediately.

⊗ TIPS

Here we've served the steak with pancetta wrapped just on the sides, but if you prefer you can cover the steak with pancetta entirely, making a parcel with the meat and rosemary hidden inside.

You can cook the steak without the wine – just fry it or grill it under a high heat.

Remember to use a good-quality wine for your steak . . . if it's not good enough to drink, then it's not good enough to cook with!

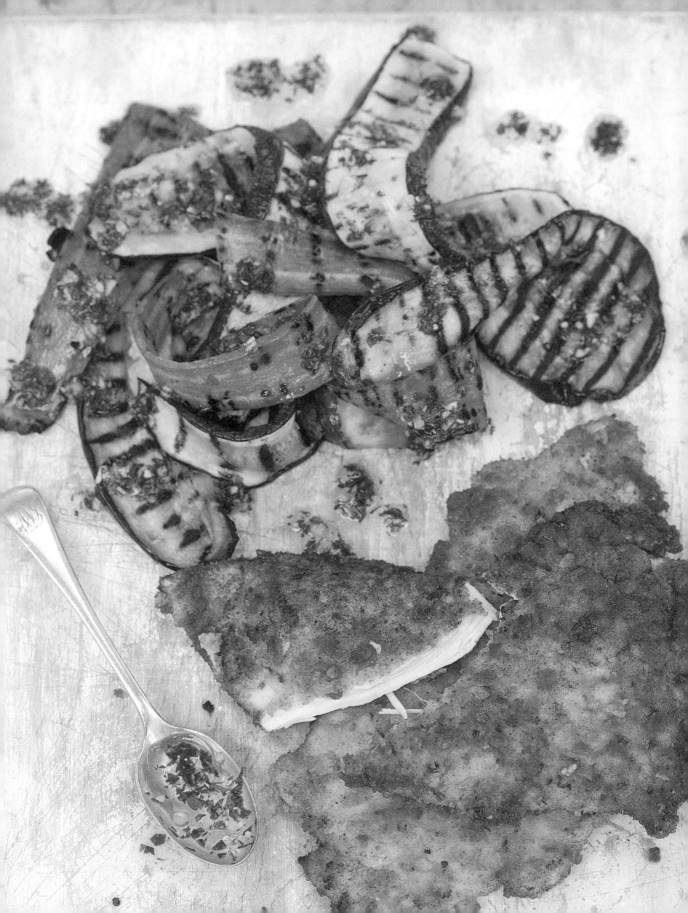

Crunchy Breaded Chicken

COTOLETTE DI POLLO

These breaded chicken pieces make for soothing comfort food and bring back lovely memories for all of us. When we arrived home after the long journey back from Italy, Nonna Luisa would have a bowl of *pastina* in chicken broth waiting for us, followed by some *cotolette*. This is a traditional Milanese dish, although most regions of Italy have their own version – and of course everyone thinks theirs is the best! We like to serve this with Multi-Coloured Griddled Vegetables (page 208), drizzled with a little Classic Pesto (see page 117).

Serves: 4
Preparation time: 15 minutes
Cooking time: 10 minutes

2 chicken breasts, skin removed

2 medium eggs, preferably free-range or organic

fine salt and freshly ground black pepper

150g breadcrumbs

1 tablespoon dried herbs (parsley, rosemary or thyme)

4 teaspoons salted butter, plus extra if needed

olive oil

lemon wedges, to serve

Slice each chicken breast horizontally across the middle to make 4 fillets. Cover with cling film and, using a meat mallet or a rolling pin, pound each fillet until it is about 0.5cm thick.

In a shallow dish, beat the eggs and season with salt and pepper. Place the breadcrumbs on a plate and mix in the herbs. Take each piece of chicken and dip it first in the egg, then coat in the herby breadcrumbs.

Melt the butter with the oil in a frying pan over a medium heat. When frothy, cook the chicken for about 2 to 5 minutes on each side, until cooked through. You may need to cook the chicken in batches, depending on the size of your pan – use a teaspoon of butter and olive oil per chicken piece. (Use more butter or a little oil if the breadcrumbs have soaked it up before you turn the chicken, or if you want your cotolette to be extra crunchy.) Serve with the lemon wedges.

 TIPS

For a spicy kick, add a teaspoon of chilli flakes to the bread-crumbs or serve with sweet chilli sauce.

For a healthier option, drizzle the chicken in a little olive oil and bake in an oven heated to 180°C/350°F/gas 4 for 20 minutes, until cooked through.

Speedy Chicken with Salty Parma Ham and Fresh Sage

SALTIMBOCCA

Salty Parma ham flavoured with the woody taste of sage turns a plain chicken breast into something rather special. The literal translation is 'jumps into your mouth' and we think it's because this dish is so quick to cook and so delicious that you will want to gobble it up straight away!

Serves: 4
Preparation time: 10 minutes
Cooking time: 15 minutes

2 chicken breasts, skin removed

fine salt and freshly ground black pepper

8 slices of Parma ham

8 fresh sage leaves

1 tablespoon olive oil

a wine glass of white wine

Slice each chicken breast horizontally across the middle to make 4 fillets. Cover with cling film and, using a meat mallet or a rolling pin, pound each fillet until it is about 1cm thick. Season both sides with salt and pepper.

Place 2 slices of Parma ham on top of each chicken piece. Top with 2 sage leaves and weave a toothpick through to secure them in place.

Heat the oil in a frying pan over a medium heat and fry the chicken for about 2 minutes on each side, until cooked through. Transfer to serving plates.

Add the wine to the pan, reduce over a high heat for 1 minute and then serve the chicken with the juices drizzled over.

 TIPS

Emi loves to sprinkle on a little fennel pollen with the salt and pepper as it really brings out the flavours of the chicken, sage and Parma ham, but you could also use ground fennel seeds.

This is how saltimbocca *is served in our region of Italy, Emilia Romagna, but for an extra level of luxury, place a slice of cheese between the chicken and the Parma ham, roll into a log, secure with a toothpick and cook in the oil and white wine. Bear in mind that the cooking time may be longer. We use caciotta cheese, but you could use Taleggio, Brie or even a thin slice of Cheddar.*

Lemon Chicken

POLLO AL LIMONE

This is another quick dish that Mum used to give us when we were little. We always serve it with a big mound of plain rice to soak up all the fresh, zesty juices. It's so tasty you'll want to lick your plate clean (and we sometimes do when no one is looking!).

Serves: 6
Preparation time: 5 minutes
Cooking time: 15 minutes

2 tablespoons olive oil

1 tablespoon salted butter

800g chicken breasts, skin removed, chopped into 2.5cm pieces

juice of 1 large lemon

1 teaspoon cornflour

1 teaspoon brown sugar

1 organic chicken stock cube

fine salt and freshly ground black pepper

a handful of chopped fresh parsley, to garnish

Heat the oil with the butter over a medium heat. Fry the chicken for about 10 minutes, turning regularly to brown all over.

Put the lemon juice, cornflour and sugar in a small bowl and mix together to form a smooth paste. Crumble the stock cube into 250ml hot water, then add to the chicken with the paste. Stir to coat the chicken and simmer for 2 to 4 minutes, until the sauce thickens. If the sauce becomes too thick, loosen it with a splash of water. Season with salt and pepper, and serve scattered with the chopped parsley.

 TIPS

Add a splash of white wine to give it some extra flavour.

If you find the sauce is too sharp, stir through a tablespoon of fresh cream or cream cheese.

Marsala Chicken

POLLO AL MARSALA

Marsala is a staple in every Italian kitchen. It is similar to sherry and when reduced it becomes rich and syrupy. We like to serve this with mashed potatoes or wild rice to absorb the tasty juices.

Serves: 4
Preparation time: 5 minutes
Cooking time: 20 minutes

1 tablespoon salted butter

1 tablespoon olive oil

4 chicken breasts, skin removed, washed and patted dry

100ml good-quality hot chicken stock

150ml Marsala wine

fine salt and freshly ground black pepper

1 teaspoon cornflour

Heat the butter and oil in a heavy-bottomed frying pan over a medium heat and fry the chicken for 2 minutes on each side, until browned all over.

Add the stock and Marsala and simmer for 10 to 15 minutes, turning the chicken to coat in the sauce. Remove the chicken from the sauce once cooked and set aside, covered in tin foil to keep warm. Season the sauce with salt and pepper.

Mix the cornflour with 1 tablespoon of water until dissolved and stir into the sauce. Continue cooking the sauce, stirring for 2 minutes, until it has thickened. Serve the chicken with the sauce poured over the top.

TIPS

If you don't have Marsala, you can use brandy, sherry or cognac.

When you reduce the sauce, try throwing in some lovely button mushrooms and sliced shallots with a little fresh thyme.

Hunters' Hotpot

POLLO ALLA CACCIATORA

How the Italians do *coq au vin*! This was one of our Nonna Luisa's classics. She said it originated from the farmers and huntsmen who would cook with whatever ingredients they had available. They kept hens and, with basic vegetables from their garden, would make this simple meal for a special occasion. It is a great dish for a large dinner party, but it is also good if you are on a budget.

Serves: 4–6
Cooking time: 50 minutes

1 tablespoon salted butter

1 tablespoon olive oil

8 chicken thighs or drumsticks, skin left on

1 onion, peeled and finely chopped

2 carrots, peeled and finely chopped

2 sticks of celery, finely chopped

1 clove of garlic, peeled and finely chopped

fine salt and freshly ground black pepper

2 sprigs of fresh rosemary, leaves picked and finely chopped

a wine glass of red or white wine

1 x 400g tin good-quality plum tomatoes

1 tablespoon tomato purée

a handful of chopped fresh parsley, to garnish

Heat the butter and oil in a large heavy-based pan and cook the chicken pieces skin-side down for approximately 10 minutes, turning to brown them all over. When the skin is a lovely golden colour, add the chopped vegetables. Season with a little salt and pepper, stir in the rosemary and cook for about 5 minutes. There may be a lot of fat in the pan from the chicken skin, but don't worry as the vegetables will absorb most of this and it adds extra flavour. Stir in the wine and cook for about 2 minutes. The aim is to burn off the alcohol, leaving just a hint of the lovely wine flavour.

Add the tomatoes and tomato purée. Cover with a lid and simmer on a low heat for about 30 minutes, until the chicken is cooked through. If the sauce starts to dry out, add a ladleful of water or stock. Serve sprinkled with chopped fresh parsley.

 TIPS

This also works well made with lamb or rabbit pieces – add a handful of thyme along with the rosemary.

For a lighter version, drain off the fat from the pan once the chicken has browned.

Italians play several varieties of the card game 'briscola'. It can be played between two people, or more commonly, two sets of partners.
Our parents love to play this game when we are all home together.

A Leftover Feast

VITELLO TONNATO

After a six-course Christmas lunch (which usually lasts about six hours!), we always have loads of leftovers – often taking us through to New Year. This is a great traditional sauce that Italians love to serve with cold roast meats. You may think that a tuna sauce is an odd addition to sliced meat, but don't dismiss it until you've tried it. Think of it as Italian surf 'n' turf ...

Makes enough to serve: 8–10
Preparation time: 5 minutes

1 x 185g tin tuna in oil, drained

4 tablespoons good-quality mayonnaise

2 tablespoons lemon juice

1 tablespoon white wine vinegar

3 tablespoons extra virgin olive oil

2 tablespoons capers, drained

optional: 2 or 3 anchovy fillets

thinly sliced cold meats, to serve

chopped capers and chopped fresh flat-leaf parsley, to garnish

Place all the ingredients (except the meat) in a food processor and blitz to a smooth consistency. Pour over the sliced meat and garnish with a few capers and a little parsley.

 TIPS

You can prepare this sauce in advance and keep it in the fridge for up to 3 days.

This is also great served over prawns as an alternative to a traditional prawn cocktail, or as a dip for raw vegetables.

Pork Tenderloin in the Oven

FILETTO DI MAIALE

If you fancy a change from the traditional Sunday roast, this makes a great alternative. As an added bonus, it's quick, easy and doesn't involve endless pots and pans!

Serves: 4
Preparation time: 15 minutes
Cooking time: 1 hour

600g pork tenderloin

fine salt and freshly ground black pepper

2 tablespoons olive oil

200ml white wine

1 large white onion, peeled and quartered

2 carrots, peeled and roughly chopped

2 sticks of celery, roughly chopped

1 organic vegetable stock cube

optional: capers, to garnish

Preheat the oven to 180°C/350°F/gas 4.

Season the pork with salt and pepper. Heat the oil in a casserole (or heavy ovenproof dish with a lid) over a high heat. When the oil is very hot, add the pork. It will spit, so be careful. Sear the meat until brown all over.

Add the wine, onion, carrots, celery, crumbled stock cube and 500ml cold water, then transfer the casserole to the oven and cook for 40 minutes.

Remove the vegetables from the casserole, cover with tin foil and set aside. Transfer the pork to a chopping board and cover with tin foil. Leave to rest for 5 minutes. Meanwhile, put the casserole back on the stove over a high heat to reduce the sauce a little.

Slice the pork into thick slices and serve, scattered with the capers, if using, on a bed of the cooked vegetables. Drizzle with some of the sauce.

 TIP

Serve this with wild rice, or you could add a few potatoes or parsnips to the casserole before putting it in the oven – a great one-pot meal!

Pork Medallions with Onion, Apple and Cider

FILETTO DI MAIALE CON CIPOLLA, MELA E SIDRO

Every Saturday, at Casa Chiappa, the men leave the house at the crack of dawn to do 'man's work'. They chop wood for the winter, tinker in the shed and generally potter about. At around 4 p.m. they come back in, rosy-faced and muddy, expecting a hearty, meaty meal. This dish only takes 30 minutes; meaning us girls can spend the whole day doing whatever we want.

Serves: 4
Preparation time: 15 minutes
Cooking time: 15 minutes

300g wild rice

1 tablespoon olive oil

1 white onion, peeled and finely chopped

1 tablespoon plain flour

500g pork tenderloin, cut into 2.5cm-thick medallions

a splash of cider or white wine

1 apple, peeled, cored and coarsely grated

½ an organic chicken stock cube

½ teaspoon French mustard

fine salt and freshly ground black pepper

1 tablespoon single cream

In a large pan of salted boiling water, cook the rice. To check the rice is cooked, taste a few grains; it should be soft but with a slight bite.

Meanwhile, heat the oil in a large frying pan over a medium heat and fry the onion for about 4 minutes, until soft and translucent. While the onion is cooking, put the flour in a shallow bowl and coat the pork with the flour.

Add the pork to the pan and seal the meat on both sides. Dissolve the crumbled stock cube into 100ml boiling water, then add to the pan with the cider, apple and mustard. Cook for 5 minutes, and then turn over the pork to cook on the other side for 5 minutes. Season with salt and pepper, stir through the cream and serve over the drained rice.

⊗ TIPS

Instead of using cider or wine, try making this with a splash of brandy or cognac for a richer flavour.

Emi likes to add a sprig or two of fresh thyme – never be afraid to use herbs to adjust the taste of a dish.

This dish also works really well with pork chops.

Mum's Braised Beef in Red Wine Stew

STRACOTTO

A perfect example of how a few simple ingredients can create a powerful combination of flavours. We sometimes eat this the next day, when the flavours have soaked in, making it even more delicious. Serve the stew with mashed potatoes or polenta to soak up all the lovely juices.

Serves: 4–6
Preparation time: 10 minutes
Cooking time: 2 hours
20 minutes

50g salted butter

1kg lean beef joint

1 onion, peeled and sliced

2 cloves of garlic, peeled and crushed

1 organic beef stock cube

750ml full-bodied red wine (e.g. Merlot)

1 tablespoon tomato purée

2 bay leaves

8 black peppercorns

In a large casserole dish, melt the butter over a high heat and brown the beef on all sides for about 5 minutes. Add the onion and garlic to the pan and cook for 2 minutes – be careful not to burn the garlic.

Dissolve the stock cube in 200ml boiling water and add to the pan with the wine, tomato purée, bay leaves and peppercorns. Bring to a slow boil, then cover with a lid, lower the heat and simmer for 2 hours, until the meat is tender.

Remove the meat from the pan and set aside, covered in tin foil to keep warm. Remove and discard the bay leaves.

Blitz the juices with a handheld blender and reduce over a high heat for 10 minutes. Serve the meat with the rich wine sauce.

 TIPS

For an even richer sauce, Mum sometimes adds a handful of porcini mushrooms along with the stock.

If you think it needs it, you can use a teaspoon of cornflour to thicken the sauce. Stir it into the reduced sauce and cook for 2 minutes.

We love to use this as the filling for anolini (see page 58).

Nonna's Hearty Sausage Stew

COTECHINO IN UMIDO

After a long walk on a crisp day, we love to come back to this hearty winter-warmer of a dish. Traditionally it is made with lentils rather than potatoes, but when we were children we didn't like lentils, so Nonna Luisa adapted the recipe and we've never gone back to the original.

Serves: 4–6
Preparation time: 15 minutes
Cooking time: 30 minutes

1 tablespoon olive oil

2 medium onions, peeled and diced

2 tablespoons tomato purée

500g cotechino or good-quality coarse-textured sausages, skin removed, chopped into 2.5cm pieces

1kg potatoes, peeled and cut into large pieces

1 organic chicken or beef stock cube

1 teaspoon cornflour, if needed

fine salt and freshly ground black pepper

In a heavy-bottomed pan (large enough to hold about 2 litres of water), heat the oil over a medium heat. Fry the onion with the tomato purée for about 5 minutes, until lightly golden. Stir in the sausages and cook for 2 to 3 minutes, until browned all over.

Add the potatoes and crumbled stock cube and cover with 800ml cold water. Bring to the boil, cover with a lid, then lower the heat and simmer for about 20 minutes, until the potatoes are cooked through. They are ready when they fall off the blade of a knife easily. If the sauce is a little dry, loosen it with a splash of water; if it seems too liquid, thicken with the cornflour. Season, to taste, with salt and pepper. Serve in bowls.

 TIPS

Romina likes to add 200g button mushrooms along with the potatoes.

This is an excellent dish to make a day or two in advance as it tastes even better when the flavours have had a chance to mingle. Keep in the fridge until ready to serve, then heat through, making sure the sausages are hot in the middle.

Bags of Goodness

PESCE E PATATE ALL'ITALIANO

This is a delicious and healthy dish that is really easy to prepare – and there's no washing-up either! The baking parchment keeps in all the tasty juices, but it also keeps all those fishy smells out of your kitchen. You can try it with any type of fish, but we love using fresh white fish like sea bass or halibut. It's important that you slice the potatoes really thinly, so they cook through at the same time as the fish.

Serves: 4
Preparation time: 15 minutes
Cooking time: 25 minutes

600g small new potatoes, cut very finely into 0.5cm slices

4 x 170g sea bass fillets, skin removed, washed and patted dry

fine salt and freshly ground black pepper

1 teaspoon fennel pollen

1 lemon, cut into thin slices

4 spring onions, trimmed and cut into equal pieces

300g fresh asparagus spears, woody ends removed, chopped into equal pieces

1 tablespoon extra virgin olive oil

Preheat the oven to 200°C/400°F/gas 6.

Cut 8 pieces of baking parchment into 35cm x 35cm squares. Place 4 pieces next to each other on the work surface. Arrange a quarter of the potatoes in the middle of each square and place a fish fillet on top. Season generously with salt and pepper, and sprinkle with a little fennel pollen. Place 2 or 3 lemon slices on top of each fish fillet and scatter the spring onions and asparagus over and around. Drizzle with a little oil.

Top each pile with a second piece of parchment and, starting at one corner, twist the edges all the way round to seal the parcel. Make sure there aren't any gaps for the steam to escape, otherwise the potatoes won't cook properly. Place on a baking tray and cook in the oven for 25 minutes.

Serve the parcels straight onto plates so you retain all the lovely juices.

⊗ TIPS

If you can't find fennel pollen, you could use crushed fennel seeds, or we sometimes use dried oregano or chopped fresh dill instead.

You can substitute the asparagus with green beans.

Aubergine and Mozzarella Bake

MELANZANE ALLA PARMIGIANA

This is layered like lasagne but made with aubergine instead of pasta. It is a typical dish made all over Italy, but we like to think it originates in Parma. The men in our family love meat, but they'll happily eat this veggie dish regularly. It can be served hot or cold, and also as a starter or side dish to accompany *Saltimbocca* (see page 166).

Serves: 6
Preparation time: 1 hour
Cooking time: 40 minutes

1kg aubergine, sliced thinly lengthways

fine salt

5 tablespoons olive oil

1 x quantity of Classic Tomato Sauce (see page 96)

½ teaspoon cayenne pepper

400g freshly torn mozzarella cheese

100g freshly grated Parmesan cheese

Place a layer of aubergine slices on a plate. Sprinkle with salt and cover with kitchen paper. Continue layering the aubergine in this way, finishing with kitchen paper. Weigh the aubergines down using something heavy, like a saucepan filled with water, and leave for 30 minutes so that the aubergine can release its bitter juices.

Preheat the oven to 180°C/350°F/gas 4.

Brush each aubergine slice with a little oil and heat a frying pan over a medium heat. Fry the aubergine, a few slices at a time, until cooked through and golden on both sides. Add a little more oil to the pan if needed. Once cooked, place the aubergine on some kitchen paper to absorb any excess oil.

Reheat the Classic Tomato Sauce and stir through the cayenne pepper. Cover the bottom of a 30cm x 20cm baking dish with 2 tablespoons of the sauce. Top with a layer of aubergine and lightly spread with 4 tablespoons of sauce. Sprinkle generously with mozzarella and Parmesan. Repeat these layers (aubergine, sauce, mozzarella and Parmesan) until you have used all the aubergine, finishing with a layer of sauce and Parmesan (no mozzarella).

Cook in the oven for 40 minutes, or until golden brown and cooked through.

 TIP

For a healthier option, lightly brush the aubergine slices with oil and cook them on a griddle instead of frying them.

PANCAKES
Frittelle

This recipe is so simple: 1 cup of flour, 1 cup of milk, 1 egg. It can be used to make breakfast pancakes (add some blueberries to the batter) or you can fill the pancakes with ricotta sauce, roll them up and bake them covered in Basic White Sauce (see page 81).

Makes: 6–10 pancakes, depending on the size of your frying pan
Preparation time: 20 minutes
Cooking time: 15 minutes

1 cup (120g) plain flour

1 cup (240ml) milk

1 medium egg, preferably free-range or organic

a knob of unsalted butter, if needed

In a medium bowl, whisk together the flour, milk and egg until you have a smooth batter. The batter shouldn't be too thick, so add a splash more milk if needed.

Heat a good-quality non-stick frying pan (15—20cm in diameter) over a high heat. (A good pan is the secret to successful pancakes!) Pour a ladleful of the batter into the pan and tilt the pan from side to side to spread the batter out to the edges. Leave the pan on the heat for 2 to 3 minutes, until the pancake has set. Flip over the pancake and cook on the other side for about 2 minutes. Repeat with the rest of the batter. If you find the pancakes are sticking to the pan, melt a little butter in the pan before adding the batter.

Classic Pancakes Stuffed with Spinach and Ricotta

PANZEROTTI TRADIZIONALI

We loved these as children and would help Mum stir the mixture and roll them up – we called them 'roly-polys'! They're also a great way of using up any leftover filling from making tortelli (see page 57).

Serves: 4
Preparation time:
  Pancakes: 20 minutes
  Basic White Sauce:
  10 minutes
  Filling: 10 minutes
  Assembling: 10 minutes
Cooking time: 20 minutes

1 x quantity of pancake batter (see opposite)

a knob of butter, to grease

1 x quantity of Basic White Sauce (see page 81)

a splash of milk, if needed

for the filling

240g spinach leaves, washed and patted dry

125g ricotta cheese

125g mascarpone cheese

60g freshly grated Parmesan cheese, plus extra for the topping

fine salt and freshly grated black pepper

freshly grated nutmeg, to taste

Steam the spinach in a large covered saucepan with a little water for about 5 minutes, until the spinach has wilted. Remove from the heat, drain and leave to cool (you can speed up the cooling process by running cold water over the spinach). When the spinach is cool enough to handle, squeeze to remove all the water. Place the spinach in a bowl, mix with the cheeses and season with salt, pepper and a little nutmeg.

Preheat the oven to 180°C/350°F/gas 4. Make the pancakes (see opposite). For 4 people you will need 6 pancakes.

Grease an ovenproof dish with butter. Spread each pancake with 2 tablespoons of the filling, right up to the edges. Roll up the pancakes and place in the prepared dish. Don't worry if there is space between each pancake, it's actually good to leave a little room for the white sauce to spread around them. (If you are making this for a dinner party, keep the pancakes in the fridge until your guests are ready to eat before continuing with the method.)

Reheat the white sauce, as it will have gone cold and hard – loosen it with a little milk if needed. Pour over the pancakes and sprinkle with Parmesan. Cook in the oven for 15 minutes, then grill for 5 minutes, to brown the top.

⊗ TIPS

If you're short of time, make this using ready-made cannelloni. For 4 people, you will need to double the quantity of the filling. Fill 12 cannelloni and cook for approximately 25 minutes (or as directed on the packet) in an oven heated to 180°C/350°F/gas 4, then place under the grill for 5 minutes.

Miki likes to pour a layer of Classic Tomato Sauce (see page 96) over the pancakes before the white sauce.

Salmon, Ricotta and Leek Pancakes

PANZEROTTI GALLESI

Mum created this recipe to make a change from the classic spinach and ricotta version (see page 195) and we love the sweetness of the caramelized leeks with the creaminess of the filling. It's so easy to make and brilliant to freeze, so you can have it ready, *pronto*, whenever you fancy.

Serves: 4
Preparation time:
  Pancakes: 20 minutes
  Basic White Sauce:
  10 minutes
  Filling: 15 minutes
  Assembling: 10 minutes
Cooking time: 20 minutes

30g salted butter, plus
extra to grease

1 tablespoon brown sugar

1 leek, finely chopped

250g ricotta cheese

120g smoked salmon,
finely chopped

fine salt and freshly ground
black pepper

1 x quantity of pancake batter
(see page 194)

½ quantity of Basic White
Sauce (see page 81)

freshly grated nutmeg, to taste

a splash of milk, if needed

Preheat the oven to 180°C/350°F/gas 4.

Melt the butter and sugar in a frying pan over a medium heat. Add the leeks and cook gently for about 4 minutes, until the leeks have softened and the sugar has caramelized. Remove from the heat and leave to cool for 5 minutes. Transfer to a bowl, mix with the ricotta and salmon, and season with salt and pepper.

Make the pancakes (see page 194). For 4 people you will need 6 pancakes. Reheat the white sauce and season with a little nutmeg – loosen it with a splash of milk if needed.

Grease an ovenproof dish with a little butter. Divide the ricotta and salmon mixture between the pancakes and spread it right up to the edges. Roll up the pancakes and place in the prepared dish. Don't worry if there is a little space between each pancake, it's actually good to leave room for the white sauce to spread around them. Pour the white sauce over the pancakes and cook in the oven for about 20 minutes, until the sauce is bubbling, then place under a preheated grill for 5 minutes to brown the top.

⊗ TIPS

Mum always tops this dish with a sprinkling of good old Cheddar cheese. It makes the sauce extra rich and creamy.

You can freeze the pancakes after you've rolled them but before covering with the Basic White Sauce. Defrost fully before cooking.

Sides, Soups, Salads & Dressings

Sides

If you're looking for the healthiest meals in the book, then you're in the right chapter. Side dishes are often made in Italy to accompany the *secondo piatto*, and we've brought together a few of our most popular dishes. Our favourite side dish is probably the Crunchy Shredded Roasted Cabbage with Parmesan and Breadcrumbs (see page 200), which makes an appearance whenever we cook a Sunday roast.

Soups

Who doesn't love a hearty soup? In fact, a lot of these soups were probably the first meals we ate as children. Mum would often add little *pastina* (small pasta) to Minestrone (see page 215), and you have to try our Pasta Reale (see page 219) – it's a winner with all the family and we often joke that it should be called Little Lamb's Tails since we live in Wales!

Salads and Dressings

During summers spent in Italy we will often serve a simple piece of cold meat with a salad of incredibly fresh sun-kissed vegetables – there's nothing better on a hot day. And while lots of men are not salad lovers, these are all favourites of Dad's, so we hope the men in your life will enjoy them, too.

Crunchy Shredded Roasted Cabbage with Parmesan and Breadcrumbs

CAVOLO CROCCANTE

Cabbage is a brilliant accompaniment to a roast dinner but it doesn't have to be served steamed. This is the Chiappa way! It's cheesy, crunchy and very Italian – what could be better than that?

Serves: 6
Preparation time: 10 minutes
Cooking time: 40 minutes

1 Savoy cabbage, core removed and finely shredded

5 tablespoons olive oil

40g freshly grated Parmesan cheese

20g breadcrumbs

fine salt and freshly ground black pepper

Preheat the oven to 180°C/350°F/gas 4.

Arrange the cabbage in an even layer in a large baking tray. Pour over the oil and toss to coat the cabbage.

Scatter over the Parmesan and breadcrumbs, and season with salt and pepper. Use your hands to mix together, making sure the cabbage is evenly coated.

Cook in the oven for 30 to 40 minutes, until the cabbage has crisped up. After 15 minutes of cooking, stir the cabbage around so that it cooks evenly.

 TIP

For a healthier option, leave out the Parmesan and breadcrumbs and just drizzle with olive oil.

Stuffed Baked Courgettes

ZUCCHINE RIPIENE

This is so simple but it's ALWAYS a winner! Like lots of Italian recipes, this takes just a few basic ingredients, and combines them to produce something truly delicious. We love the crunchy texture of the breadcrumbs and Parmesan cheese.

Serves: 2–3
Preparation time: 10 minutes
Cooking time: 30 minutes

3 courgettes, sliced lengthways, and deseeded

100g breadcrumbs

100g freshly grated Parmesan cheese

1–2 medium eggs, preferably free-range or organic

1 clove of garlic, peeled and finely chopped

a handful of chopped fresh parsley

fine salt and freshly ground black pepper

2 tablespoons olive oil

Preheat the oven to 180°C/350°F/gas 4. Bring a large pan of water to the boil (it needs to be big enough for the courgettes to fit comfortably).

In a bowl, mix together the breadcrumbs and Parmesan with one of the eggs, the garlic and parsley. If the mixture is too crumbly, add the second egg until it starts to stick together. Season, to taste, with salt and pepper.

Blanch the courgettes in the boiling water for about 2 minutes. Remove from the water, pat dry and place on a baking tray. Spoon the breadcrumb mixture into the courgettes. Drizzle with the oil and bake in the oven for 20 to 30 minutes, until golden brown.

 TIPS

If you want to make the courgettes extra cheesy and crunchy, grate a little extra Parmesan over the top before you bake them.

This filling can be used to stuff other vegetables like peppers, onions and aubergine.

Italian 'Roasties' with Rosemary

PATATE AL FORNO CON ROSMARINO

Our Nonna Luisa always cooked her potatoes this way. They are crispy, crunchy and delicious. These are served in abundance at the *feste* in the neighbouring towns and villages in Italy throughout August. Once you try this recipe, there will be no turning back.

Serves: 4
Preparation time: 10 minutes
Cooking time: 20 minutes

2 tablespoons olive oil

3 sprigs of fresh rosemary, leaves picked and finely chopped

1kg potatoes, peeled and cut into 1cm cubes

fine salt and freshly ground black pepper

Heat the oil in a frying pan over a high heat. Add the rosemary and potatoes and cook, turning regularly, for about 10 to 20 minutes, until golden and crispy all over.

Using a slotted spoon, remove the potatoes from the oil and drain on kitchen paper. Season with salt and pepper and serve.

 TIPS

It's important to ensure your potatoes are cut into 1cm cubes – if the pieces are larger or unevenly chopped they won't cook through at the same time.

These are delicious fried with 100g chopped pancetta.

We often sprinkle rosemary powder on top of the potatoes. Pick fresh rosemary leaves and dry them in a low oven for 20 minutes. Blitz to a fine powder in a food processor and store in an airtight jar. You'll be amazed how much you will use this seasoning - it's great with breaded chicken or veal, Nonno's Mini Sausage Rolls (see page 149) or sprinkled over soups.

Cheesy Leeks

PORRI CON FORMAGGIO E BURRO

Maybe it's the Welsh leeks that make us love this recipe so much! It's great as a side dish, but it can also be eaten as a light meal. Nonna Luisa used to cook this for our Dad, and he still says hers was the best.

Serves: 3–4 people as a side dish, 2 as a light main
Preparation time: 10 minutes
Cooking time: 40 minutes

500g leeks, trimmed, halved and sliced lengthways

40g salted butter, plus extra to grease

60g freshly grated Parmesan cheese

3–4 medium eggs, preferably free-range or organic

fine salt

Bring a large pan of salted water to the boil and cook the leeks for 5 to 10 minutes, until soft and translucent. Remove from the heat, drain and leave to cool (you can speed up the cooling process by running cold water over the leeks – make sure you drain them thoroughly).

Grease the base of a large lidded frying pan with a little butter. Arrange a third of the leeks in an even layer over the bottom of the pan. Dot with a third of the butter and sprinkle with a third of the Parmesan. Repeat these layers twice more.

Cook the leeks over a low heat for 20 to 30 minutes, until the cheese is bubbling and the base is starting to turn crispy.

Crack the eggs on top of the leeks and sprinkle the yolks with a little salt. Cook with the lid on for 5 minutes or until the eggs are cooked to your liking.

 TIP

You can substitute the Parmesan with grated Cheddar for a more British version.

Multi-Coloured Griddled Vegetables

VERDURE DI TUTTI I COLORI

Serves: 8
Preparation time: 40 minutes
Cooking time: 20–30 minutes

2 aubergines, sliced
thinly lengthways into
0.5cm-wide strips

fine salt and freshly ground
black pepper

3 tablespoons olive oil,
plus extra to griddle

a handful of finely chopped
fresh parsley

2 cloves of garlic, peeled
and crushed

4 carrots, peeled and
sliced thinly lengthways
into 0.5cm-wide strips

2 courgettes, sliced
thinly lengthways into
0.5cm-wide strips

This is a beautifully colourful dish, and a tasty way of cooking vegetables. You can serve it as a starter or as a side dish with Cotolette (see page 165). We make large supplies for our annual Italian Picnic to provide something healthy to go with the vast amounts of food we make and eat! It's great as it can be prepared a day in advance and eaten cold.

Prepare the aubergine by salting the slices (see page 193).

Put the oil, parsley and garlic in a bowl and mix together.

Heat a griddle over a medium-high heat. Lightly brush the carrots and courgettes with a little oil and cook on the griddle for about 2 minutes on each side. Repeat with the aubergine slices.

Pile the cooked vegetables on a serving plate, with a drizzle of the parsley and garlic oil between each layer. Serve warm or leave to cool.

Grated Carrot Salad

INSALATA DI CAROTE

Serves: 4–6
Preparation time: 5 minutes

8 carrots, peeled and
finely grated

juice of 1 lemon

fine salt and freshly ground
black pepper

olive oil, to drizzle

a few chopped walnuts

This is a quick-fix side salad that Mum often prepares when we are in Italy during the summer. Even though it only uses a few ingredients, it's delicious and crunchy and always goes down well on a hot day.

Mix all the ingredients together in a bowl and garnish with a handful of chopped fresh chives . . . *troppo facile!*

Juicy Peas in a Rich Tomato Sauce

PISELLI IN UMIDO

Serves: 4–6
Preparation time: 5 minutes
Cooking time: 15 minutes

fine salt and freshly ground
black pepper

1 tablespoon olive oil

1 small onion, peeled and
finely chopped

1 clove of garlic, peeled and crushed

1 x 400g tin good-quality plum
tomatoes, blitzed to a purée

400g frozen peas

1 organic chicken stock cube

Even though we're Italian, we still love a traditional British Sunday roast – alternated with Pizza Sundays, of course (see page 143). But we like to bring a little hint of Italy to every mealtime and this recipe is a delicious healthier alternative to traditional buttered peas. It will keep in the fridge for a couple of days too.

Heat the oil in a large pan over a medium heat and fry the onion for about 4 minutes, until soft and translucent. Stir in the garlic and cook until it starts to turn golden – be careful not to let it burn.

Pour in the puréed tomatoes, peas and crumbled stock cube. Stir and simmer for 10 minutes. Season, to taste, with salt and pepper.

Sweet Italian Peppers

PEPERONATA

Serves: 4–6
Preparation time: 15 minutes
Cooking time: 40 minutes

fine salt and freshly ground
black pepper

3 tablespoons olive oil

1 onion, peeled and finely chopped

3 peppers (green, red and yellow)
each deseeded and finely sliced

1 clove of garlic, peeled and crushed

1 x 400g tin good-quality
chopped tomatoes

1 teaspoon caster sugar

chopped fresh parsley, to garnish

Romina loves peppers and she'll happily eat a large helping of this on its own! It's a great way to bring a splash of colour to the table.

Heat the oil in a large frying pan over a medium heat. Cook the onion, peppers and garlic for about 5 minutes, until the onion is translucent and the peppers are soft. Be careful not to burn the garlic.

Add the tomatoes and sugar and bring slowly to the boil. Lower the heat and simmer for 30 minutes, stirring occasionally. Season, to taste, with salt and pepper and sprinkle with parsley to garnish.

Celery Soup

ZUPPA DI SEDANO

Miki couldn't believe this soup contained only celery and no potatoes, as it's so deliciously thick and tasty. Mum's good friend Lizzie taught us this recipe when we were all on a mad mission to be super-healthy for the wedding. It's a brilliant detox meal but is also a comforting soup in the winter.

Serves: 4
Preparation time: 5 minutes
Cooking time: 1 hour

1 onion, peeled and quartered

10 sticks of celery, roughly chopped

1 organic vegetable stock cube

fine salt and freshly ground black pepper

Put the onion and celery in a large pan and cover with 1.5 litres water. Add the crumbled stock cube, place over a high heat and bring to the boil. Reduce the heat, cover with a lid and simmer for about 1 hour, until the celery is soft. Blend the soup until smooth, adding extra water if needed and season with salt and pepper.

 TIP

Mum likes to stir through a tablespoon of cream cheese just before serving, or you could sprinkle with a little rosemary powder (see the Tips on page 204).

Hearty Vegetable Soup

MINESTRONE

This is a classic Italian soup eaten in the Chiappa household from infancy, as it's a great way to get children eating vegetables. Nonno Pino's generation would have made this with vegetables that were a little past their best, meaning that nothing went to waste. You can use any vegetables but aim for a mix of four or more. We tend to use earthy vegetables like carrots, onions, leeks and celery. It's a fantastic soup to make in bulk and freeze – just push it out of its container and defrost in a saucepan over a low heat. We love to eat it with pastina added near the end of cooking (see Tips).

Serves: 6–8
Preparation time: 15 minutes
Cooking time: 30 minutes

2 onions, peeled and chopped into 1cm pieces

olive oil

1 large sweet potato, peeled and chopped into 1cm pieces

1 large leek, chopped into 1cm pieces

2 courgettes, chopped into 1cm pieces

4 carrots, peeled and chopped into 1cm pieces

2 sticks of celery, chopped into 1cm pieces

4 large tomatoes or 1 x 400g tin good-quality plum tomatoes

2 tablespoons tomato purée

1 organic chicken or vegetable stock cube

fine salt and freshly ground black pepper

freshly grated Parmesan cheese, to serve

In a large saucepan, soften the onion in a little olive oil for 2 to 3 minutes. Add the rest of the vegetables, tomato, tomato purée and crumbled stock cube. Cover with water to about 4cm above the vegetables. Bring to the boil over a high heat, then reduce to a simmer. Cover with a lid and cook for 20 to 30 minutes, until the vegetables are cooked through. When you can pierce the vegetables easily with a fork, they are ready.

The soup can either be left chunky or blitzed with a blender. Season with salt and pepper and serve with lots of Parmesan sprinkled over the top.

 TIPS

For a more substantial meal, 200g pastina (small pasta) or rice can be added 15 minutes before the end of cooking (but don't blitz it!).

We each have a favourite way to adapt this basic recipe. Miki loves to add borlotti beans or lentils to her version, whereas Emi cannot go without pastina. Romina often adds a pinch of chilli along with the vegetables to give it some extra heat.

We also like to use Ortolina instead of tomato purée. It's a concentrate made up of lots of different veggies and you can find it in good Italian delis and online.

Chicken Broth

BRODO DI GALLINA

Every generation of Chiappas and Ferrari-Lanes grows up on this. It's what Mum gave us if we were ever feeling poorly. It is such a versatile dish – a simple stock you can serve hot as a clear consommé, add rice or *pastina* with lots of freshly grated Parmesan, or turn into Pasta Reale (see opposite).

Serves: 8–10
Preparation time: 15 minutes
Cooking time: 5 hours 30 minutes

1kg boiler chicken or chicken pieces (wings, thighs or legs – NOT breast)

1 large onion, peeled

2 carrots, peeled

2 sticks of celery

optional: a small bunch of fresh parsley

fine salt

5 black peppercorns

Place the chicken pieces, vegetables and parsley, if using, in a large saucepan. Cover with 2.5 litres of cold water. Sprinkle with a little salt and the peppercorns. Bring to the boil over a medium heat. As it starts to boil, remove any foam that comes to the surface with a large, flat spoon. Cover with a lid, lower the heat and simmer slowly (so that the surface of the broth is hardly moving) for 5 hours.

Strain the broth, discarding the vegetables, herbs, bones and meat and leave to cool completely. Any fat will rise to the surface and harden as it cools so it can be removed easily. The broth should be clear.

 TIPS

Freeze in individual plastic containers so you always have a portion ready. You can cook it straight from frozen.

Mash the cooked carrots with a fork and add a little broth to them and you have a simple, delicious and nutritious meal for babies.

Pasta Reale in Chicken and Chilli Broth

PASTA REALE IN BRODO

This is probably our all-time favourite recipe! We used to LIVE on this as students at university. It's speedy and simple – our version of chicken soup when we're feeling ill or instead of beans on toast. Quick, easy, filling and super-tasty! Our Nonno Pino ate Pasta Reale as a child in Pilati. They couldn't afford the meat to make anolini (see page 58) and so this was their substitute.

Serves: 1
Preparation time: 5 minutes
Cooking time: 10 minutes

½ an organic chicken stock cube or 500ml Chicken Broth (see opposite)

1 medium egg, preferably free-range or organic

fine salt and freshly ground black pepper

a handful of freshly grated Parmesan cheese, plus extra to serve

a handful of breadcrumbs

optional: ¼ teaspoon dried chilli flakes

Before you start, you should have your chicken stock or broth bubbling on the stove. Boil 500ml water and stir in the stock cube until it has dissolved, or bring the chicken broth to the boil.

Crack the egg in a bowl and whisk with a pinch of salt and pepper. Add the Parmesan and breadcrumbs and press together to form a ball of dough.

Remove the stock from the heat and hold a cheese grater over the pan. Push the dough through the large teeth of the grater and allow the tails of 'pasta' to drop directly into the boiling broth. *The 'pasta' is cooked instantly.

Serve in a bowl with lots of fresh Parmesan on top and a sprinkling of chilli flakes, if desired.

 TIPS

* Be careful: if your cheese grater is sharp, use the back of a spatula to push the dough through.

It goes without saying that homemade chicken broth would improve this meal, but a good-quality chicken stock cube is a great alternative when you're in a hurry.

Nonna's Lentil Pasta Stew

MINESTRA DI LENTICCHIE E PASTA

This is somewhere between a pasta dish and a soup. It is packed full of goodness and slow-releasing energy to keep you full all afternoon. We like to use *conchiglie* (shell pasta) as the lentils get trapped in them so you get a mouthful of different flavours and textures. Nonna Luisa used to add potatoes to this dish to make sure Uncle Laz was really full, but we prefer the lighter version!

Serves: 3–4
Preparation time: 10 minutes
Cooking time: 1 hour

1 tablespoon olive oil

1 large onion, peeled and roughly chopped

200g dried Puy lentils

1 clove of garlic, peeled and finely chopped

100ml red wine

1 organic vegetable stock cube

4 tablespoons tomato purée

optional: ¼ teaspoon chilli powder

fine salt and freshly ground black pepper

150g dried pasta (we like to use *conchiglie* or fusilli)

freshly grated Parmesan cheese, to serve

Heat the oil in a saucepan over a medium heat and fry the onion for about 4 minutes, until soft and translucent. Add the lentils and garlic and stir to coat in the oil. Pour in the wine and keep stirring for 2 minutes. The aim is to burn off the alcohol, leaving just a hint of the lovely wine flavour.

Cover with 1.5 litres of cold water, and add the crumbled stock cube, tomato purée and chilli powder, if using. Season with salt and pepper and stir for 1 minute. Simmer for about 45 minutes, until the lentils are tender but firm to the bite.

Add the pasta to the stew and cook until *al dente* (timings will vary depending on the type of pasta). Allow to cool slightly before serving. Serve in bowls with a generous grating of fresh Parmesan.

 TIPS

You can use other types of lentils – green or brown work well. Avoid using red lentils as they cook very quickly and could disintegrate. Always check the cooking times on the packet as all lentils vary.

Don't worry if the dish appears too 'soupy' – it will thicken as it cools.

Paola's Pasta Salad

INSALATA DI PASTA

With three hungry kids, Mum frequently needed to rustle up something quickly for us to eat. This salad was such a success that we often prepare it to eat at large family gatherings – picnics, birthday parties, christenings – as it can be made in large quantities and prepared in advance. It's delicious on a hot summer's day.

Serves: 8–10
Preparation time: 10 minutes
Cooking time: 10 minutes

450g dried penne

1 small red onion, peeled and finely chopped

1 small cucumber, finely diced

1 x 185g tin tuna in oil, drained

2 x 198g tins sweetcorn, drained

6 tablespoons good-quality mayonnaise

fine salt and freshly ground black pepper

Bring a large pan of salted water to the boil and cook the pasta until *al dente*. Be careful not to overcook the pasta as it will become mushy when cooled.

Place the onion and cucumber into a large bowl. Add the tuna, sweetcorn and mayonnaise and mix together.

When the pasta is cooked, drain it and then cool by running under cold water. Drain again well and mix with the other ingredients. Gently stir together to coat the pasta, and season with salt and pepper.

 TIPS

You can use other types of pasta for this – farfalle or rigatoni are good alternatives.

If you have any fresh thyme or parsley, chop a small bunch and stir it in at the end to add some extra flavour.

Rice Salad

INSALATA DI RISO

Mum made up this dish one summer in Italy. It is a bit like a Russian salad but uses rice instead of potatoes. It's brilliant to take on picnics, as you can prepare it in huge quantities the night before and keep it in the fridge. Everyone always asks for the recipe thinking it's very complicated, but it couldn't be easier!

Serves: 6
Preparation time: 5 minutes, plus cooling time
Cooking time: 10 minutes

250g basmati rice

1 x 220g jar mixed petit pois and baby carrots in brine, drained *

1 x 198g tin sweetcorn, drained

1 x 185g tin tuna in brine, drained

200g good-quality mayonnaise

fine salt and freshly ground black pepper

In a large pan of salted water, cook the rice until *al dente*. Be careful not to overcook it, as it will make the salad mushy. Drain and run under cold water to cool, then drain well again.

When the rice has cooled, mix in the rest of your ingredients and season with salt and pepper.

 TIPS

For a lighter option, replace the mayonnaise with 2 tablespoons of extra virgin olive oil.

* If you can't find a mixed jar of veggies, use a small tin of each.

Bean Salad with Tuna and Onion

INSALATA DI BORLOTTI CON TONNO E CIPOLLE

Quick and easy, this dish makes a substantial *antipasto* or can be served as a side salad. Nonna Luisa always used borlotti beans in summer salads and hearty winter stews. Nonno Pino would grow them in abundance and dry them so we always had a supply to use throughout the year.

Serves: 2 as an antipasto,
4 as a side salad
Preparation time: 5 minutes

1 x 400g tin borlotti
beans, drained

1 small red onion, peeled
and finely chopped

1 x 185g tin tuna in
brine, drained

1 tablespoon extra
virgin olive oil

½ tablespoon white
wine vinegar

fine salt and freshly
ground black pepper

In a bowl mix together the beans, onion and tuna. Stir through the oil and vinegar, and season to taste with salt and pepper.

 TIPS

To make this a bit more substantial, add a few chopped tomatoes.

The salad will keep for several days in the fridge, so make a bit extra and have it for lunch with some crusty bread.

A Large Farmers' Salad

CERESETO

This dish comes from a little farming town outside Bardi called Cereseto that we visit every summer. The locals hold an annual *festa* and we dance the night away to the music of the accordion players. Although it might seem like a bizarre combination of flavours, don't dismiss it until you've tried it. We often make this for the annual Italian Picnic – *La Scampagnata* – as it can be prepared the night before and is served cold.

Serves: 6–8
Preparation time: 30 minutes
Cooking time: 15 minutes

1 tablespoon olive oil

1 onion, peeled and
finely chopped

1 x 400g tin good-quality
chopped tomatoes

salt and freshly ground
black pepper

1 x 185g tin tuna in oil, drained

1 x 400g tin borlotti beans
(or butter beans), drained

3 medium eggs, preferably
free-range or organic,
hard-boiled and sliced

2 apples

juice of ½ a lemon

300g good-quality mayonnaise

optional: anchovies, olives
and capers

Heat the oil in a saucepan over a medium heat and fry the onion for about 4 minutes, until soft and translucent. Stir in the tomatoes, season with salt and pepper, and cook for 10 minutes. Remove from the heat and leave to cool.

When the tomatoes have cooled, start layering the salad in a large serving bowl. Start with the tomato sauce, followed by the tuna, beans and then the eggs. Core the apples, cut into quarters and slice thinly. Coat them in the lemon juice and layer on top of the eggs.

Spread the mayonnaise over the top of the apples and decorate with anchovies, capers and olives, if desired. Chill in the fridge until ready to serve.

 TIP

This is a great one for making with children. Mum used to give us a selection of ingredients to decorate the top. We'd have great fun making different patterns, and it looked pretty, too!

Summer Spinach Salad

INSALATA D'ESTATE

We love a fresh salad, and we usually make one with whatever ingredients we have to hand. However, Emi's new American family introduced this recipe to us when we went to Asheville in North Carolina a few summers ago, and we love the unique combination of flavours.

Serves: 3–4
Preparation time: 10 minutes

120g baby spinach leaves, washed and patted dry

100g fresh strawberries, chopped into small pieces

60g feta cheese

30g pine nuts

1 avocado, peeled, halved and stoned, cut into small pieces

3 tablespoons extra virgin olive oil

2 tablespoons white wine vinegar

Put the spinach in a serving bowl with the strawberries. Crumble over the feta. Mix together with the pine nuts, avocado, oil and vinegar, and serve. *Facilissimo!*

 TIPS

Instead of pine nuts, try using some chopped walnuts.

Emi sometimes makes this salad with chunks of pineapple instead of the strawberries.

Dressings

GREEN SALSA
Salsa Verde

This is a great sauce that simply oozes Italian cooking. It can add a kick to so many recipes – from bruschetta to meats and soup. Watch out for the powerful garlic punch! It has a sharp sweetness, which makes Emi think of it as Italy's equivalent of mint sauce.

Makes: approx. 350g
Preparation time: 5 minutes

100ml white wine vinegar
3 cloves of garlic, peeled
160ml extra virgin olive oil
25g sliced white bread
100g fresh parsley
½ teaspoon fine salt
¼ teaspoon freshly ground black pepper

Put all the ingredients in a food processor and blitz until smooth . . . *é tutto!*

 TIPS

If you find the sauce is too thick, add a little more oil to loosen it.

You can make a larger batch of this and store it in a sterilized jar topped with a layer of olive oil (see page 34). It will keep in the fridge for several weeks.

BALSAMIC GLAZE
Crema di Aceto Balsamico

Michela's mother-in-law, Ann Patching, gave us this recipe and we always have a supply of it in our kitchen. Even cheap balsamic vinegar produces a deliciously thick, gooey glaze, which tastes divine drizzled over meat, Tortelli Three Ways (see page 60) or simply some hot toast. If you make it in large quantities, you can keep it for months!

Makes: approx. 500ml
Cooking time: 1–2 hours

570ml balsamic vinegar
570ml red wine
130g dark brown sugar

Bring the vinegar and wine to the boil in a heavy-based saucepan. Lower the heat and simmer until reduced by half.

Stir in the sugar, allow it to melt slowly then increase the heat and boil vigorously until reduced by half again. Leave to cool a little before transferring to a sterilized bottle (see page 34).

 TIP

When you cook this, be prepared for a strong vinegar smell.

Flavoured Oils

We LOVE olive oil – it's a staple ingredient in our cupboard. However, we sometimes like to infuse it with different flavours for an easy way to mix things up. These oils are great for making a simple *antipasto*: pop some bread under the grill to warm and crisp up (you can even use bread that's gone a little stale as it will soften as it heats) and then dip it into your flavoured olive oil.

HOT CHILLI OIL
Olio Piccante

We can never eat in a pizzeria without Dad asking for *olio piccante*! He loves to drizzle it all over his pizza to give it an extra kick, and then he dips his crusts in it.

Makes: 250ml
Preparation time: 15 minutes
Cooking time: 15 minutes

1 x 250ml bottle of olive oil

5–10 fresh red chillies, depending on how hot you like your oil

1 teaspoon peperoncino powder or cayenne pepper

Pour the oil into a saucepan. Sterilize the bottle that you're going to keep the oil in (see page 34).

Add the chillies to the oil and heat over a medium heat for 10 to 15 minutes. Be careful not to burn the chillies, as they will leave a bitter taste in the oil. (Heating them will also kill off any bacteria.)

Let the oil and chillies cool to room temperature before transferring to the bottle.

GARLIC AND ROSEMARY OIL
Olio di Aglio e Rosmarino

Makes: 250ml
Preparation time: 15 minutes
Cooking time: 15 minutes

1 x 250ml bottle of olive oil

4 cloves of garlic, peeled

4 sprigs of fresh rosemary

Pour the oil into a saucepan. Sterilize the bottle that you're going to keep the oil in (see page 34).

Add the garlic and rosemary to the oil and heat over a medium heat for 5 minutes. Be careful not to burn the garlic or rosemary, which will make the oil taste bitter. (Heating them will also kill off any bacteria.)

Let the oil, garlic and rosemary cool to room temperature before transferring to the bottle.

Desserts

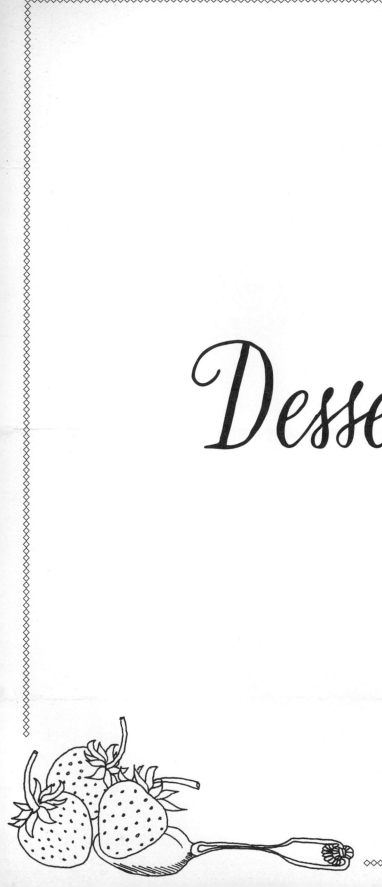

Every family has a member with a particularly sweet tooth, and we're no exception. Most Sundays, Mum will make a selection of desserts to please us all: a fruity option, something creamy, a boozy treat and, of course, a chocolaty favourite!

In this chapter, we've given a Chiappa twist to some traditional dishes. You can whip up our Tiramisù in about twenty minutes (see page 250) – ideal for that last-minute dinner party you decide to host on the spur of the moment. Or try our Italian take on the British classic bread and butter pudding (see page 259). This is one Mum has to take the credit for; she decided to make it with panettone one Christmas, and now we never make it any other way.

We've also included recipes that we've gathered together from our Nonnis' and Bis nonnis' (great-grandparents') handwritten recipes. This was no easy task as Nonna Luisa's way of writing a recipe was to list the ingredients without giving any quantities or basic instructions! Some recipes were Dad's and Laz's favourites when they were growing up, so we've made them over and over again and adapted them to ensure they are just as the boys remember.

Creamy Mascarpone Mousse with Berry Compote

CREMA DI MASCARPONE CON FRUTTI DI BOSCO

Rosanna Seghini has been head chef at the Due Spade restaurant in Bettola (Mum's hometown) for as long as we can remember. She's just retired but we managed to get hold of her recipe first. We order this every summer during our holiday and it is Romina's favourite. It can be served as a dessert in its own right, but it also makes a great accompaniment to fresh fruit salad or spread on top of our Nonno's Welsh Cakes (see page 291).

Serves: 4
Preparation time: 15 minutes
Chilling time: 30 minutes
Cooking time: 10 minutes

for the creamy mousse

2 medium eggs, preferably free-range or organic, separated

55g caster sugar

170g mascarpone cheese

for the berry compote

100g fresh strawberries, stalks removed, washed and patted dry

100g fresh raspberries, washed and patted dry

100g fresh blackberries, washed and patted dry

1 tablespoon caster sugar, plus extra to taste

Beat the egg yolks and sugar in a large bowl or free-standing electric mixer, until pale yellow and frothy. Slowly mix in the mascarpone.

In a separate bowl, beat the egg whites until they form stiff peaks. Fold the egg whites into the mascarpone mixture, until all the ingredients are well incorporated. Chill in the fridge while you make the compote.

Place the berries in a small saucepan and stir in the sugar. Heat over a low heat for 10 minutes, until the berries start to break down. Leave to cool, then add more sugar to taste.

Serve the mousse topped with some of the compote.

 TIPS

In the winter, when fresh berries are expensive and harder to find, use frozen berries.

As an alternative to the berry compote, crumble a few amaretti biscuits on top of the mousse.

Please note this contains raw egg; the mousse is not cooked.

Hot Strawberries with Ice Cream and Amaretti

FRAGOLE SALTATE IN PADELLA

This Italian recipe title can be translated as 'strawberries hopping in a pan', and it certainly is that! You don't want to cook the strawberries; you only want to heat them through, otherwise they will turn to mush. We love the hot–cold–hot sensation; it's very ooohh, ahhh, mmmmm . . .

Serves: 4
Preparation time: 5 minutes
Cooking time: 2 minutes

450g fresh strawberries

1 tablespoon unsalted butter

2 tablespoons brown sugar

½ a wine glass of brandy or cognac

4 scoops of good-quality vanilla ice cream

2 amaretti biscuits

Remove the stalks and slice the strawberries in half.

In a medium saucepan, melt the butter with the sugar until the sugar has dissolved and it's starting to bubble.

Gently place the strawberries in the pan and tip the pan from side to side to coat them in the melted butter and sugar. Immediately pour the brandy over the top and light with a match to flambé. Be careful! Give the pan a shake, until the alcohol has burned off and the flames disappear. This process should take no more than 20 seconds; avoid overcooking the strawberries, as they will start to lose their colour and become very soft.

Transfer to serving bowls and serve with a scoop of vanilla ice cream and crumble over the amaretti biscuits. Serve immediately. *Ecco! Tutto finito!*

 TIP

This dish works well with other berries, too, but remember not to cook the fruit – it just needs quickly heating through.

Puff Pastry with Creamy Mascarpone and Sweet Berries

MILLEFOGLIE CON MASCARPONE E FRUTTI DI BOSCO

This is Emi's twist on the classic Italian dessert, *millefoglie*. It is much quicker to make than the traditional version, which is often served at the many christenings and weddings we attend every summer in Italy. It's so delicious that Miki and Emi chose this for their wedding cake: a one-metre-square *millefoglie* covered with masses of fruits of the forest!

Serves: 4
Preparation time: 10 minutes
Cooking time: 20 minutes

icing sugar, to dust

250g ready-rolled puff pastry

1 medium egg, preferably free-range or organic

120g fresh strawberries, washed and patted dry, hulled and sliced

120g raspberries, washed and patted dry

120g blueberries, washed and patted dry

2 tablespoons caster sugar

250g mascarpone cheese

zest of 1 lemon

1 vanilla pod, slit lengthways and seeds scraped out

2 tablespoons double cream

Preheat the oven to 200°C/400°F/gas 6.

On a work surface dusted with icing sugar, roll out the pastry until it is 0.5cm thick. Using a sharp knife, cut the pastry into 8 rectangles about 7cm x 10cm. Cut out the centre of 4 of the pastry rectangles, so you are left with 1cm-wide frames.

Beat the egg and brush over the 4 complete rectangles. Place a pastry frame on top of each and prick the base inside the frame with a fork. This will prevent it rising up during cooking.

Place the pastry rectangles on a baking tray lined with parchment paper and cook in the oven for 15 to 20 minutes (this may vary depending on the pastry; check the packet for cooking instructions), until the sides have risen and the pastry is golden brown. Set aside and leave to cool.

Meanwhile, place the berries in a bowl, sprinkle with the caster sugar and set aside.

In a medium bowl, mix the mascarpone, lemon zest and vanilla seeds, until well combined. Stir in the cream.

When the pastry cases have cooled, if the base has risen a little inside the frame, push the pastry back down. Spread a generous layer of mascarpone cream across the base of the pastry, top with a layer of berries and sprinkle with 1 teaspoon of the juice. Repeat with the rest of the pastry cases, dust with icing sugar and serve immediately.

 TIP

In the summer, juicy peaches work really well in this dessert.

Ice Cream Drowned in Coffee

AFFOGATO

The combination of hot and cold here is irresistible, and this is one of the easiest desserts going. As it's so simple, we recommend you use the finest-quality ingredients you can afford. We haven't suggested any quantities, as it's really up to you how much you would like!

Serves: as many as you need!   *Cooking time: the time it takes to brew the coffee*

good-quality vanilla ice cream

optional: amaretti biscuits, to serve

good-quality hot black coffee or espresso

Put 1 or 2 scoops of the ice cream in a small dessert bowl or cup. Crumble an amaretto biscuit over the ice cream, if you like. Pour over a little hot coffee or an espresso, and enjoy!

Boozy Custard

ZABAGLIONE

This is a real Italian classic that can be served on its own although we sometimes use it to cover our Angel Sponge Cake (see page 271). It's a bit tricky to master but well worth the effort. If it goes wrong and the eggs separate, just try again!

Serves 4   *Preparation time: 10 minutes*   *Cooking time: 15 minutes*

4 large egg yolks, preferably free-range or organic

4 tablespoons caster sugar

4 tablespoons Marsala wine, cognac or sweet white wine

In a glass bowl beat the egg yolks and sugar together until light and fluffy. Half-fill a pan with water and bring to a gentle simmer over a medium heat. Place the bowl with the egg mixture over the pan, making sure it doesn't touch the water. Add the Marsala to the egg mixture and whisk continuously until thickened: when you pull the whisk out, it should create a ribbon effect. This takes about 10 to 15 minutes.

Pour into individual glasses and serve hot or chilled. If you're chilling it, give the mixture a quick stir just before serving to prevent it from separating.

For an extra treat, place an Amaretto-soaked biscuit at the bottom of each serving glass.

Dad's Easter Dessert

DOLCE DI PASQUA

Italian mums love to pamper their sons, and we can confirm that this stereotype is true. Even when Dad was married, Nonna Luisa would take him a clean cotton hanky to his car every morning before he set off for work. Often, if Dad didn't like what Mum had cooked him for dinner, he would pop next door to Nonna's for a 'better' option! What a cheek! Every Easter, Nonna made Dad his favourite dessert – and Easter desserts are always sinful, with plenty of cream, chocolate and booze. After all, it's time to indulge after giving up all those treats for Lent, right? Us Chiappas will use any excuse . . .

Serves: 8
Preparation time: 30 minutes
Chilling time: 1 hour, or
preferably overnight

3 medium eggs, preferably free-range or organic, separated

3 tablespoons caster sugar

300ml double cream

100g whole almonds with their skins on, roughly chopped

2 tablespoons cognac

100g good-quality dark chocolate chips

2 tablespoons cocoa powder

150g amaretti biscuits, crushed

25g whole almonds

Beat the egg yolks and sugar in a large bowl or free-standing electric mixer, until light and fluffy.

In a separate bowl, beat the egg whites until they form stiff peaks. In another bowl, beat the cream until soft peaks. Fold the egg whites into the sugar mixture, and then fold in the cream.

Divide the mixture into two bowls. Into one half gently mix the chopped almonds and 1 tablespoon of the cognac. Into the other half of the mixture, add the rest of the cognac, the chocolate chips and the cocoa powder. Be careful not to stir too much, as the mixture needs to be light and airy.

Spread half the almond mixture into the bottom of a glass serving dish approximately 22cm in diameter and 10cm deep. Sprinkle with one third of the crushed amaretti and half the whole almonds. Layer with all of the chocolate mixture followed by another third of the amaretti. Finish with the remaining almond mixture and top with the rest of the amaretti and the whole almonds. Chill in the fridge for at least 1 hour, and preferably overnight.

 TIPS

If you don't have amaretti biscuits, use any light crumbly biscuit (digestives work a treat!).

Please note this contains raw egg.

Elsa's Chocolate and Biscuit Dessert

DOLCE D'ELSA

This recipe belonged to our Great-aunt Elsa (Nonno Pino's sister). Elsa was the coolest great-aunt ever! Aged eighty, she would still vault over the fence to pick some lettuce rather than go the long way round. And when we stumbled in from a nightclub at 4 a.m., she'd be up, offering us a plate of pasta or a glass of limoncello – such a legend! Nonno loved this dessert so much that when he got married, he asked Elsa to share the recipe with his wife. And now it has passed through the generations to us. It's a very simple dish, and one that Romina often made at university for her chocoholic housemates; not only will it please chocolate-lovers but it's also very thrifty!

Serves: 6–8
Preparation time: 30 minutes
Chilling time: 1 hour, or preferably overnight

180g unsalted butter, at room temperature

180g caster sugar

4 medium eggs, preferably free-range or organic, separated

180g hot chocolate powder or cocoa powder

200g Marie or Rich Tea biscuits, roughly broken

500ml double cream

Cream the butter and sugar in a large bowl or free-standing electric mixer until light and fluffy. It's important that the butter is at room temperature to achieve a smooth consistency. Add the egg yolks and continue to mix until well combined. Stir in the chocolate powder and mix until incorporated.

In a separate bowl, beat the egg whites until they form stiff peaks. Carefully fold into the chocolate mixture, keeping in as much air as possible so it is light and fluffy. Fold in the broken biscuits, making sure they are evenly distributed.

Spoon the mixture into a serving dish. (You can either choose a large dish or individual bowls. If you're making separate portions, allow 3 large tablespoons per person.) Chill in the fridge for at least 1 hour, until set.

When you're ready to serve, whisk the cream in a bowl until thick and spread over the top of the chocolate.

TIPS

This is great for dinner parties as you can make the chocolate base the day before and leave it to set overnight.

Please note this contains raw egg.

Tiramisù

TIRAMISÙ

There are hundreds of recipes for tiramisù and every Italian will have an opinion on what is the 'right way' to make this classic dessert. We love our version: super quick to prepare, it's almost foolproof and can be made the night before a party and chilled in the fridge. A delicious, creamy, coffee treat! It looks really special if you make it in a glass dish, so you can see the layers.

Serves: 6–8
Preparation time: 25 minutes
Chilling time: 1 hour, or
preferably overnight

3 medium eggs, preferably free-range or organic, separated

3 tablespoons caster sugar

250g mascarpone cheese

2–3 tablespoons cocoa powder

250ml Marsala wine

250ml good-quality strong black coffee

1 x 200g packet of sponge finger biscuits

Beat the egg yolks with the sugar in a bowl or use a free-standing electric mixer until light and fluffy. In a large bowl, beat the egg whites until they form stiff peaks. Add the mascarpone to the egg-yolk mixture and mix to combine, and then fold in the egg whites. Don't over-mix, you want to keep this nice and fluffy.

Spread a thin, even layer of the mixture over the bottom of a serving dish approximately 22cm in diameter and 10cm deep. Using a fine sieve, sprinkle a little cocoa powder over the top.

Put the Marsala into a shallow dish, and do the same with the coffee in another dish. One by one, quickly dip each side of the biscuits first in the Marsala and then in the coffee. Don't let them absorb too much liquid, as they can get rather soggy. Place a neat layer of the soaked biscuits on top of the cocoa powder.

Repeat this process, layering the creamy mixture, cocoa powder and soaked sponge biscuits, finishing with a layer of the creamy mixture. Each creamy layer should just cover the biscuits; don't spread it too thickly. You ideally want 4 or 5 layers. Lightly dust with more cocoa powder and then chill in the fridge for at least 1 hour, and preferably overnight.

⊗ TIPS

We recommend that you use strong coffee for this recipe. We prepare ours in an Italian moka pot – when you use it the smell of coffee brewing is delicious.

Mum likes to make individual portions in jam jars so they can be stored in the fridge easily. You'll need to crumble the biscuit layers so that they fit inside.

Please note this contains raw egg.

Pears Poached in Wine

PERE E VINO

We love to eat this after a Sunday roast as it's light and very refreshing. Plus, you can pretend you're being healthy by eating fruit – even though it's soaked in red wine! This is extra delicious served with the Creamy Mascarpone Mousse on page 237.

Serves: 6
Preparation time: 10 minutes
Cooking time: 30 minutes

125g caster sugar

500ml red wine

½ teaspoon ground cinnamon

optional: 2 star anise

6 hard pears, peeled, cored and sliced in half lengthways, stalks intact

mascarpone cheese, to serve

Put the sugar, wine, 500ml water, the cinnamon and the star anise, if using, in a saucepan. Stir together and heat over a medium heat until the sugar has dissolved.

Add the pears, making sure they are fully submerged. Bring to the boil, then lower the heat and simmer for 10 minutes. Remove from the heat and leave the pears to cool in the liquid. This should take approximately 30 minutes.

Remove the pears from the liquid and place in a serving dish. Boil the wine mixture over a high heat until reduced by half and leave to cool a little before pouring over the pears. Serve with a large spoonful of mascarpone.

 TIPS

This can also be made with white wine, although it will look less dramatic!

For a healthier, less sweet version, halve the quantity of sugar.

Roasted Peaches with Orange Syrup

PESCHE DOLCI AL FORNO

Emi came across this while on her honeymoon in southern Tuscany. Chef David Hangan at the *La Bandita* hotel cooked it for her and we've recreated it here. The flavour combination of roasted peach and sweet orange syrup is simply divine and brings back wonderful memories of summers in Italy spent eating juicy ripe peaches!

Serves: 4
Preparation time: 5 minutes
Cooking time: 30 minutes

40g unsalted butter, at room temperature

4 juicy peaches

8 tablespoons caster sugar, plus extra to coat the pears

8 tablespoons freshly squeezed orange juice

Preheat the oven to 180°C/350°F/gas 4.

Rub the butter over the peaches and coat them in sugar. Place in a baking dish and cook in the oven for 30 minutes.

While the peaches are cooking, put the 8 tablespoons of sugar and orange juice in a small pan. Bring to the boil over a medium heat and continue to boil until it thickens and begins to froth. Turn off the heat and allow the syrup to continue to thicken. Serve the peaches drizzled with the syrup.

 TIPS

Traditionally, this is made with white peaches, but any peach will do – the juicier, the better! Or why not try it with other fruit – pears would work very well.

A scoop of vanilla ice cream will take this to another level . . .

Layered Mocha Torte

TORTA DI MOKA

Having been brought up surrounded by coffee, this dessert naturally made a regular appearance. When we were little, Mum made it without alcohol; but the older we got, the boozier it became! If you don't like Amaretto or brandy, you can use another liqueur like Marsala, sherry or a sweet wine.

Serves: 8–10
Preparation time: 40 minutes
Chilling time: 30 minutes,
preferably 1 hour
Cooking time: 5 minutes

4 medium egg yolks, preferably free-range or organic

175g unsalted butter, at room temperature

175g caster sugar

8 heaped tablespoons good-quality instant coffee

100ml brandy

100ml Amaretto

1 x 200g packet of sponge finger biscuits

100g flaked almonds

300ml double cream

Cream the egg yolks, butter and sugar in a large bowl or free-standing electric mixer. It's important that the butter is at room temperature to achieve a smooth consistency. In a small bowl, dissolve half the coffee in 3 tablespoons of hot water and stir into the mixture.

In another bowl, dissolve the remaining coffee in 100ml hot water. Pour into a shallow dish with the brandy and Amaretto. Stir together and set aside.

Line a 10cm x 20cm loaf tin with cling film, leaving enough hanging over the edges to seal your cake over the top of the tin.

One by one, quickly dip each side of the biscuits into the coffee-and-liqueur mixture. Don't let them absorb too much liquid, as they can get rather soggy. Line the bottom and sides of the loaf tin, laying the biscuits side-by-side, like soldiers.

Spoon half the creamed mixture into the tin and top with a layer of soaked biscuits. Spoon over the rest of the creamed mixture and finish with another layer of soaked biscuits. Wrap the cling film over the top and chill in the fridge for at least 30 minutes, preferably 1 hour.

When ready to serve, toast the flaked almonds in a dry pan over a medium heat for about 5 minutes, until golden brown. Turn out the cake onto a serving plate and remove the cling film. In a small bowl, whip the cream until light and fluffy and spread over the cake until completely covered. Decorate with the flaked almonds to create a 'hedgehog' effect. Slice and serve.

 TIPS

For a different effect (or if you have run out of time!), sprinkle crushed almonds over the top.

Please note that this contains raw egg.

Paola's Panettone Pudding

PANETTONE DOLCE DI PAOLA

This is the Italian version of British bread and butter pudding. Mum made up this recipe after we were given vast amounts of panettone one Christmas, and it's now one of our most requested puddings.

Serves: 8
Preparation time: 20 minutes
Cooking time: 1 hour

25g unsalted butter, at room temperature, plus extra to grease

6 medium eggs, preferably free-range or organic

700ml milk

70g caster sugar

450g panettone, cut into 1.5cm slices

4 tablespoons apricot jam or marmalade

icing sugar, to dust

Preheat the oven to 160°C/325°F/gas 3. Grease a 30cm x 20cm ovenproof dish with a little butter.

In a bowl, mix together the eggs, milk and sugar until well combined – there's no need to whisk.

Butter the slices of panettone, then layer the slices in the prepared dish, overlapping them slightly. Using a sieve to make sure there are no lumps, cover the panettone with the egg mixture.

Place the panettone dish in a large roasting tray and place in the oven. Carefully fill the roasting dish halfway up with hot water to create a bain marie. (The hot water will help keep the temperature even during cooking.) Cook for 1 hour, until the egg mixture has set. Remove from the bain marie.

Before the panettone cools, warm the jam in a small saucepan over a medium heat. Spread a thin layer over the top of the panettone. Allow to cool a little before dusting with icing sugar.

 TIP

For a healthier option, you can leave the panettone unbuttered when you layer it in the dish.

Cakes and Biscuits

Who doesn't love a good cake? It's very rare that our kitchen is without some sort of baked creation . . . especially when Romina, the resident baker, is about.

We've pulled together our favourite recipes for this chapter – ones that Mum usually bakes for Dad on a weekly basis, and some that we do for birthdays when we have Uncle Laz's family over from next door for a slice of cake and a glass of prosecco. Some of the photographs in this book were taken on Romina's birthday this year, so the Almond Cake (see page 276) was baked and decorated, and then everyone tucked in!

For us, the most classically Italian cake is the Ultimate Jam Tart on page 272. Our *nonne* always had one in their cupboards and it evokes lovely memories of Italy. It's the kind of cake that easily lasts for a week, so it's always on hand for breakfast, dessert or if you have an unexpected guest.

If you're after something easy-peasy and a little bit fun, get involved with the Coconut Truffles (on page 284); they'll take you all of 15 minutes to make and can be eaten almost immediately.

Living in Wales has inevitably given some of our recipes a Welsh twist. Our Nonno Morwood is the only Welsh part of our family and was a baker by trade. He taught us his famous Welsh Cake recipe (see page 291), which he served in his busy café in Bridgend. Miki likes to eat them with a dollop of mascarpone and a little orange zest for a taste of Italy.

Cakes always make people smile, so have a go, and enjoy!

Classic Italian Sponge Cake

CIAMBELLA

This is Dad's favourite cake and Mum often throws one together on a Sunday evening so that he can have it for breakfast during the week. It's one of the easiest cakes to make and takes next to no time. You just need to weigh your eggs and use the same amount of the other ingredients. And as it's so moist, it will last for several days if you keep it in a cake tin.

Makes: 12–15 slices
Preparation time: 10 minutes
Cooking time: 40 minutes

5 medium eggs, preferably free-range or organic

Weigh the eggs in their shells and use the same weight of the following ingredients:

unsalted butter (approx. 250g), at room temperature, plus extra to grease

self-raising flour (approx. 250g)

caster sugar (approx. 250g)

½ teaspoon baking powder

2 tablespoons milk

Preheat your oven to 180°C/350°F/gas 4. Grease a 20cm bundt cake tin generously with butter.

Mix all the ingredients in a large bowl or free-standing electric mixer, until well combined, light and fluffy. It's important that the butter is at room temperature to achieve a smooth consistency.

Scrape the mixture into the prepared tin and bake in the oven for 40 minutes, until golden brown. Do not open the oven door, as the cake will sink! To check if the cake is cooked, insert the tip of a sharp knife into the centre and when it comes out clean, it is ready.

Turn out onto a wire rack and leave to cool.

 TIPS

Emi likes to add the zest from a lemon to the cake mixture for a little hint of lemon flavour.

For an instant lemon drizzle cake, boil the juice of a lemon with 3 tablespoons of sugar in a small saucepan for 5 minutes. Pour this on top of the cake as soon as it comes out of the oven and, hey presto!

Cinnamon Sponge Cake with Apples

TORTA DI MELE

This is one of the cakes that would be waiting for us at our Auntie Elsa's when we arrived in Italy for the summer holidays. The smell of cinnamon and apple would waft through her house, and whenever we make it, we are transported back there. It is a great alternative to a traditional apple pie.

Serves: 8–10
Preparation time: 25 minutes
Cooking time: 1 hour

100g unsalted butter, plus extra to grease

200g plain flour, plus extra to dust

800g sweet apples (such as Pink Lady), peeled, cored and sliced into 1cm wedges

zest and juice of 1 lemon

2 medium eggs, preferably free-range or organic

200g brown sugar

1 teaspoon baking powder

1 teaspoon ground cinnamon

½ teaspoon grated nutmeg

½ teaspoon fine salt

200ml milk

1 teaspoon vanilla extract

Preheat the oven to 180°C/350°F/gas 4. Grease a 25cm round tin with butter and dust lightly with flour.

Place the apple in a bowl and pour over the lemon juice. Set aside.

In a small saucepan, melt the butter over a low heat. Meanwhile, beat the eggs and sugar in a large bowl or free-standing electric mixer, until pale yellow and fluffy. Add the melted butter to the egg mixture and stir to combine. Add all the remaining ingredients and mix together until well incorporated.

Gently stir in the apples and lemon juice, making sure the apple pieces are evenly distributed throughout the cake batter. Scrape into the prepared tin and bake for 50 minutes to 1 hour, until golden brown. To check if the cake is cooked insert the tip of a sharp knife into the centre and when it comes out clean, it is ready. Leave to cool for 10 to 15 minutes before slicing and serving.

 TIP

This is delicious served with crème fraîche or a big spoonful of mascarpone cheese.

Caterina's Chocolate Loaf

TORTA DI CATERINA

Emi learned how to make this when she was nannying in Lugano, on the Swiss border. One of the children, Caterina, was coeliac and her mum made this special cake. Being a nanny to three children doesn't leave much time for baking and this recipe is not only quick but is guaranteed to bring a big smile to your face!

Serves: 6–8
Preparation time: 15 minutes
Cooking time: 30 minutes

150g good-quality dark chocolate

100g caster sugar

200g almonds, very finely chopped

2 large eggs, preferably free-range or organic

125g unsalted butter, at room temperature, plus extra to grease

icing sugar, to serve

Preheat the oven to 180°C/350°F/gas 4.

Break the chocolate into small pieces and place in a heatproof bowl that fits snugly on top of a saucepan. Half-fill the pan with water to create a bain marie and bring to a gentle simmer. Place the bowl containing the chocolate on top, making sure it doesn't touch the water (or it will get too hot). Stir with a metal spoon until the chocolate has melted.

In a medium bowl, mix together the sugar, almonds and eggs. Add the melted chocolate and butter and stir until well combined. It's important that the butter is at room temperature to achieve a smooth consistency.

Grease a 23cm x 12cm loaf tin with a little butter. Scrape the mixture into the tin and bake for 30 minutes.

Remove from the oven and leave to cool in its tin for 15 minutes. Turn out from the tin, dust with icing sugar and serve in thick slices.

 TIP

We always use almonds in this recipe, but it will work with any nuts as long as they are finely chopped to approximately the size of half a peppercorn. Don't use ground or roughly chopped nuts.

Angel Sponge Cake

TORTA DEGLI ANGELI

The recipe for this light-as-an-angel sponge cake was given to us by one of the 'aunties' from our Italian–Welsh community. It's lighter and fluffier than a traditional sponge cake because it's made mainly with potato flour. As the baker of the family, Romina often makes this for our birthdays, as she likes to get a little creative with the decoration! (See Tip.)

Serves: 10–12
Preparation time: 30 minutes
Cooking time: 55 minutes

unsalted butter, to grease

10 medium eggs, preferably free-range or organic, separated

340g caster sugar

140g potato flour

60g self-raising flour

½ teaspoon baking powder

zest of 1 lemon

1 teaspoon vanilla extract

icing sugar, to dust

Preheat the oven to 180°C/350°F/gas 4. Grease a 25cm round tin with butter and line with baking parchment. If the tin doesn't have high sides, extend the baking parchment above them to about 20cm high.

Beat the egg yolks and sugar in a large bowl or free-standing electric mixer, until pale yellow and fluffy. In a separate bowl, beat the egg whites until they form stiff peaks.

Sieve the flours and baking powder into the egg-yolk mixture and fold gently to combine. Add the lemon zest and vanilla extract and slowly mix until well incorporated, then fold in the egg whites.

Scrape into the prepared tin and cook for exactly 55 minutes. Do not open the oven door, as the cake will sink! Remove the cake from the oven and turn out onto a wire rack to cool. Dust with a little icing sugar.

 TIP

Romina loves to go one step further and cover the top of the cake with Zabaglione (see page 244).

Ultimate Jam Tart

CROSTATA

This is a classic Italian jam tart and if you walk into any bakery in northern Italy you are guaranteed to see one on the counter. Every grandmother, aunt and sister has their own recipe – Mum has about five different versions in her scrapbook! This recipe has taken the best bits from each to make the Ultimate Jam Tart. Take a trip to The College House (Michela and Dan's coffee shop in Cardiff), where it's often on the menu. Perfect for afternoon tea, or breakfast with a pot of coffee.

Serves: 10–15 (depending on the size of the slices!)
Preparation time: 15 minutes
Chilling time: 30 minutes
Cooking time: 45 minutes

225g unsalted butter, chilled, plus extra to grease

450g plain flour, plus extra to dust

5 medium egg yolks, preferably free-range or organic

170g caster sugar

zest of 1 lemon

1 teaspoon vanilla extract

1 teaspoon baking powder

a splash of rum, Amaretto or milk, if needed

370g jam, in a flavour of your choice

Preheat the oven to 180°C/350°F/gas 4. Grease a 28cm round shallow baking tin with a little butter.

Mix the butter and flour in a large bowl or free-standing electric mixer, until it resembles fine sand. Add the egg yolks, sugar, lemon zest, vanilla extract and baking powder. Keep mixing until well combined and the mixture starts to form a dough. If it seems a little dry, add a splash of rum, Amaretto or milk. Cover the dough with cling film and rest in the fridge for 30 minutes.

Cut off one quarter of the dough and set aside. On a floured work surface, roll out the remaining pastry until it's 0.5cm thick and large enough to line the prepared tin, ensuring the base and sides are completely covered. (If the dough is a little crumbly, push in any stray pieces of dough when you've lined the tin.)

Spoon the jam into the pastry case and spread to form an even surface. Fold over any excess pastry around the sides to create a 2cm-border. On a floured surface, roll out the remaining quarter of the dough and cut into long strips, about 2.5cm wide. (Use a pasta cutter to create a crinkled edge if you have one.) Use the strips to create a lattice effect over the top of the jam.

Cook in the oven for 30 to 45 minutes, until the pastry is golden brown. Leave to cool in its tin before serving with a cup of freshly brewed tea . . .

 TIPS

In Italy this is often made with plum or prune jam; the slight bitterness of the fruit is offset by the sweet pastry.

Another, rather indulgent, option is to substitute Nutella for the jam . . . obviously the best option when you're on a diet.

Rose Cake

TORTA DELLE ROSE

Elisabetta, a family friend who lives next door to us in Italy, introduced us to this cake. It is a cross between a Chelsea bun (without the raisins) and a croissant. It's great for breakfast and best eaten very fresh. It's not difficult to make, but you need plenty of patience, as there's a lot of waiting around, and a free-standing electric mixer if possible.

Serves: 12
Preparation time: 50 minutes
Resting time: 3 hours
Cooking time: 50 minutes

200ml milk

10g fresh yeast

1 teaspoon runny honey

500g plain flour, plus extra to dust

4 medium eggs, preferably free-range or organic

80g caster sugar

2 teaspoons fine salt

1 teaspoon vanilla extract

100g unsalted butter, at room temperature, plus extra to grease

optional: apricot jam, to serve

for the filling
150g unsalted butter, at room temperature

150g caster sugar

optional: 2 teaspoons ground cinnamon or 3 tablespoons Nutella

Gently warm the milk in a small saucepan over a low heat. Dissolve the yeast in the milk and stir in the honey. Place the flour in a bowl and stir in the milk mixture until well combined.

In a separate bowl, beat 3 of the eggs. Add the sugar, salt and vanilla extract, and beat together. Add to the flour mixture and mix together for 10 to 15 minutes, until it forms a wet dough. It will be very wet – almost like a cake batter.

Divide the butter into 6 pieces. One at a time, use your hands to mix the butter pieces into the flour mixture, making sure each one is well combined before adding the next. Knead for a further 10 minutes to form a wet, sticky dough.

Grease a 28cm round baking tin with butter. Transfer the dough to the prepared tin and cover with cling film. Leave the dough in a warm place for 2 hours, or until it has doubled in size.

While the dough is rising, prepare the filling. Beat the butter and sugar in a large bowl or free-standing electric mixer, until pale, light and creamy. (At this point you can mix in the cinnamon or Nutella to make cinnamon or chocolate rolls.)

When the dough has doubled in size, remove from the tin and place on a well-floured surface. Roll out the dough until it is roughly 60cm x 40cm and 5cm thick. Spread the filling evenly over the rectangle, right up to the edges. With the long side facing you, roll the dough over and over to form a sausage shape. Using a sharp knife, cut into 12 slices, each about 4cm thick.

Re-grease the baking tray and line with parchment. Place the rolls in the tray with plenty of space between them to allow for rising. Rest in a warm place for 1 hour, until doubled in size.

Preheat your oven to 180°C/350°F/gas 4. When the rolls are ready to cook, beat the remaining egg and brush lightly over them. Cook for 45 to 50 minutes, until golden brown. If you like, brush the cooked rolls with a thin layer of apricot jam to give them an extra gloss and to add a subtle flavour.

Almond Cake

TORTA ALLE MANDORLE

Our Aunt Lili gave us the recipe for this light and moreish cake. Romina likes to call it the 999 Almond Cake because the quantities are nine of everything, but we're certain it would be good in emergencies, too.

Serves: 8–10
Preparation time: 15 minutes
Cooking time: 1 hour
15 minutes

unsalted butter, to grease

9 medium eggs, preferably free-range or organic, separated

9oz (255g) caster sugar

9oz (255g) almonds, skin on, finely ground

½ teaspoon gluten-free baking powder or ½ a packet of *Lievito Pane degli Angeli* (see page 19)

juice and zest of 1 lemon

for the filling
500g mascarpone cheese

100g icing sugar, plus extra to dust

400g fresh raspberries, washed and patted dry

Preheat the oven to 180°C/350°F/gas 4. Grease two 23cm round baking tins with a little butter and line with baking parchment.

Beat the egg yolks and sugar in a large bowl or free-standing electric mixer, until light and fluffy. In a separate bowl, beat the egg whites until they form stiff peaks. Fold the egg whites into the sugar mixture then add the almonds, baking powder, lemon juice and zest, and mix gently until well combined.

Scrape the mixture into the prepared tins and bake in the oven for 30 minutes. Lower the heat to 150°C/300°F/gas 2 and cook for a further 30 minutes, until the top is golden brown. Do not open the oven door, as the cakes will sink! To check if the cakes are cooked insert the tip of a sharp knife into the centre and when it comes out clean, they are ready. Remove from the tins and cool on a wire rack.

While the cakes are cooling, beat the mascarpone and icing sugar in a large bowl, until well incorporated and the consistency of soft butter.

When the cakes have cooled, spread the top of one cake with the mascarpone icing. Smooth over to create an even surface. Starting from the edge, arrange the raspberries over the mascarpone. Place the second cake on top. (If you find that one of your cakes has sunk, turn it over so it is concealed in the middle of the cake!) Dust with icing sugar.

 TIPS

Raspberries don't stay fresh for long, so this ideally needs to be eaten the same day. Omit the raspberries if you need the cake to last a little longer.

If you prefer, you can make this in one large 30cm cake tin and use the mascarpone mixture on the top, or eat the cake on its own!

Crunchy Italian Almond Biscuits

CANTUCCINI

Our cousin's aunt, renowned for making delicious Italian desserts, gave us this biscuit recipe. She always brings these to our annual Italian Picnic – *La Scampagnata*. They are perfect with a cup of coffee after a meal and can be made to suit your teeth – the longer you bake them, the harder they become! Cantuccini are completely addictive: you won't be able to stop eating them.

Makes: 10–12
Preparation time: 20 minutes
Cooking time: 25–40 minutes

150g unsalted butter, plus extra to grease

225g plain flour

225g almonds, roughly chopped

225g caster sugar

a pinch of fine salt

1 teaspoon baking powder

2 medium eggs, preferably free-range or organic

1 teaspoon cognac

1 teaspoon vanilla extract

optional: zest of 1 small orange

icing sugar, to dust

Preheat the oven to 180°C/350°F/gas 4. Grease a 28cm round shallow cake tin with a little butter and line with baking parchment.

Melt the butter in a small saucepan over a medium heat. Remove from the heat and leave to cool a little.

In a large bowl, mix together the flour, almonds, sugar, salt and baking powder. Add the eggs, cognac, vanilla extract and orange zest, if using. Stir together until well combined.

When the butter has just cooled, add to the flour mixture (if the butter is too warm it might start cooking the eggs). Mix together until it starts to form a dough – it will be quite crumbly.

Press the dough into the base of the cake tin with the palms of your hands, making sure you squash it right into the corners. It should cover the whole of the base in an even layer about 3cm deep.

Cook in the oven for about 25 minutes, until risen slightly and golden brown. If you remove them now, the biscuits will have a softer, chewier consistency. If you would like a harder biscuit, like traditional *cantuccini*, leave in for 10 minutes more.

Remove from the oven and turn out onto a wire rack to cool. When cool enough to handle, cut into large fingers. Sprinkle with icing sugar before serving.

 TIP

The biscuits can be stored in an airtight container for up to 2 weeks.

the College House Coffee Rules

Why is it that you can get a great cappuccino wherever you are in Italy, and yet in the UK you're more likely to be served a weak, watery instant mix, a bucket of coffee in a cardboard cup, or a scalding bitter drink?

For starters, a cappuccino should never be bitter; it should be creamy and smooth, and served in a small cup. It should be just warm enough to enjoy and never so hot that it hurts when it touches your lips. And if a cappuccino is served just right, you shouldn't need sugar to cut through any bitterness.

In the UK, so many coffee shops get it wrong: they boil their milk so that it burns the coffee, and they don't know how to clean their machines, so you end up with a bitter drink. It was a rant just like this one that led to The College House – Miki and Dan's coffee shop nestled in the heart of the student community in Cardiff. They wanted to set up a place which served a GOOD coffee – simply, with no fuss and certainly not overpriced. If people want an enormous vat of coffee, then they can pay over the odds for it; but at The College House, small cappuccinos are – as they should be – £1.

It is called The College House because it is set in the middle of the student quarter, because Miki and Dan met while at university and because Dan's background is teaching. Our motto is: *'Italian Flavour, British Style'*, and the look and feel are influenced by traditional British academic institutions. It is decorated with bookshelves, original school desks (from Mum's old school!), blackboards and old sofas. And everyone in the family has played a part in bringing it all together: Nonno Pino helped make the shelves and the display boards, and even the sign outside was handcrafted by the Chiappa men.

As for 'Italian Flavour', well, you've heard our rant about coffee! But this ethos runs throughout the entire café; all the food is made on site and we use the finest-quality ingredients from local and Italian suppliers. Before we opened, Dan was shipped to Italy to spend some time with our baker cousin, Paolo Chiappa, to learn how to make proper Italian *focaccia* (see page 146) and pizza *al trancio*. A couple of nights a week, we do a late-night session with thin-crust Italian pizzas for just £5. They are made fresh to order and are ready in around 4 minutes.

HOW TO DRINK COFFEE, 'PROPERLY' . . .

So, now that we've let you know a bit about our background, we thought we'd give you a guide to how Italian coffee should be served. (And, in true Italian style, it will no doubt spark some good debates and controversy!) However, you should obviously drink your hot drinks as you like them – and there's a perfect example of rule-breaking in our own family. Generally, you won't see an Italian drinking a cappuccino after 11 a.m. (after this, they only order espresso or a long black coffee), but our Mum loves a milky, creamy coffee in the afternoon – and Dad is always horrified!

1. CAPPUCCINO: A real Italian cappuccino should be served warm (not scalding hot), in a small cup. The coffee should be smooth and the milk should have a slight mousse-like texture. You don't need to boil your milk to get nice big frothy bubbles. Run away if you see a barista pumping the milk jug under the steam wand! Most Italians drink a cappuccino in the morning with a brioche, standing at the bar and enjoying some chit-chat with their local barista.

2. ESPRESSO An espresso is a short black coffee and it is the most popular way to drink coffee in Italy. It should be served with a good layer of *crema* on the top – the golden layer that sits on top of your coffee. If it doesn't have a *crema* layer, your coffee is likely to be sharp and bitter. The *crema* is made from oils extracted from fresh coffee beans and it gives your coffee a smoother taste. An espresso is the basis of all other coffees, so if your barista cannot get this part right, then he's starting off on the wrong foot! There is a misconception that a cappuccino or latte contains less coffee than an espresso (we often have customers in the café saying, 'Oh, no, I can't have an espresso, as that's too much caffeine for me!') but most coffees start life as a shot of espresso – a cappuccino or latte will just make it go further!

3. MACCHIATO This is an espresso with a dash of frothy milk. If you don't want to drink a straight shot of coffee but you don't want a long milky coffee either, then this is the drink for you. The verb *'macchiare'* means 'to stain', so this drink literally means an espresso, stained with a dash of milk.

4. LATTE Latte actually translates as 'milk'; it was the Americans who started to use this term to refer to a long milky coffee with a little bit of foam on the top. In Italy, you will need to ask for a *latte macchiato*, as otherwise you will get a glass of milk. Again, this should never be scalding hot, as it will burn the coffee and give a bitter taste.

5. MOCHA A mocha is a latte with a shot of chocolate syrup. Baristas will often present this in a tall glass, so you can clearly see the three layers: chocolate, coffee and milk. We serve ours with thick dark or white chocolate. It's that little bit more indulgent for when you want a real treat!

6. OUR HOT CHOCOLATE The College House serves this with several secret ingredients added – it is like nothing you've tasted before. That's all we'll say on the matter; you'll just have to come and try one!

'Our motto is:
'ITALIAN FLAVOUR, BRITISH STYLE'.'

7. HOT CHOCOLATE MOUSSE This is for all you chocolate-lovers! It is exactly what it says: a thick chocolate mousse, which you'll need to eat with a spoon. It's more like a hot chocolate dessert than a drink and has the consistency of custard. The chocolate actually contains potato starch and so the more you heat it, the thicker it becomes.

Coconut Truffles

PALLE DI COCCO

Everyone always heads straight for these when we have them at a party because they're easy finger food, look great and taste even better. They are incredibly simple to make and perfect for children's parties, too. Romina even turned the truffles into 'eyeballs' for a Halloween party!

Makes: about 50
Preparation time: 15 minutes
Chilling time: 10 minutes,
preferably 30 minutes

400g condensed milk
350g desiccated coconut

Put the condensed milk and coconut in a large bowl and mix until well combined. Using your hands, mould the mixture into walnut-sized pieces, placing them on a baking tray as you go. Place the baking tray in the fridge so the truffles can set for at least 10 minutes, preferably 30 minutes. It's not essential to chill them but it helps the truffles keep their shape.

 TIP

Shaping the truffles can be a sticky process, but do not fear: you can just lick your fingers clean at the end!

Nonna Luisa's Sweet Fried Pasta

SPRELLE / CHISURIN

Just as we eat pancakes on Shrove Tuesday, our Nonna Luisa used to make these sweet snacks before the start of Lent. We'd all look forward to one last feast before abstaining (or trying to abstain!) from sweets, chocolate and other treats. They're also great as an afternoon snack.

Serves: 8–10
Preparation time: 20 minutes
Resting time: at least 30 minutes, preferably 1 hour
Cooking time: 10–15 minutes

500g plain flour

90g caster sugar

35g unsalted butter, at room temperature

3 medium eggs, preferably free-range or organic

1 teaspoon vanilla extract

a pinch of fine salt

a splash of milk, if needed

100g lard

icing sugar, to dust

Put the flour, sugar, butter, eggs, vanilla extract and salt into the bowl of a free-standing electric mixer with the dough hook attached. Mix together on a medium speed until well combined. It should start to come together into a dough. If it's not forming a dough, use your hands to combine the mixture. You may need to add a splash of milk if the mixture is too dry. Once a dough has formed, cover with cling film and rest for at least 30 minutes, ideally 1 hour, at room temperature. It's often better for the dough to be a little dry because it will moisten while it rests. You can also make the dough by hand.

Roll out tennis-ball-sized amounts of dough until they are about 0.5cm thick, using either a pasta roller or by hand. The dough is quite crumbly but the more you work it, the easier it will become. Cut it into long ribbons, about 2cm wide, or any shape you like. Our Nonna always used to tie long strands into loose knots.

Melt the lard in a large saucepan over a medium heat. When the lard is hot, fry the pieces of dough a few at a time for 3 or 4 minutes, until they are golden brown. Using a slotted spoon, transfer to some kitchen paper to absorb the excess fat. Dust with icing sugar and serve.

⊗ TIPS

Nonna Luisa always made an incredibly large batch of these. They keep in an airtight container for several weeks, which allowed her to pull them out whenever a family member turned up unannounced.

If you don't want to use lard, you could substitute any neutral-tasting oil, such as vegetable oil, but in our opinion the traditional way is best here!

Chocolate Gooey Brownies...
Without Butter!

TORTA AL CIOCCOLATO ... SENZA BURRO!

This is a recipe that Emi experimented with while trying to lose a few pounds before the wedding. She's a total chocoholic and couldn't live without eating it, so decided that if she could come up with a brownie recipe that didn't contain any butter she'd feel a little less guilty! These brownies use apple sauce as a substitute, but you would never know the difference as they're deliciously soft and moist.

Makes: 9
Preparation time: 10 minutes
Cooking time: 20 minutes

unsalted butter, to grease

100g plain flour

25g cocoa powder

100g brown sugar

1 teaspoon baking powder

a pinch of fine salt

1 medium egg, preferably
free-range or organic

130g apple sauce

1 teaspoon vanilla extract

150g chocolate chips

Preheat the oven to 180°C/350°F/gas 4. Grease a 20cm square baking tray with a little butter.

Place all the ingredients in a large bowl and mix together until well combined. It may seem quite dry in comparison to traditional brownie mixtures, but will be fine when cooked. Scrape the mixture into the prepared baking tray and, using the back of a spoon, spread to create an even surface. Cook in the oven for 20 minutes. Leave to cool for 5 minutes before cutting into slices and devouring instantly.

 TIPS

If you want to make this even healthier, you could use wholewheat flour and leave out the chocolate chips ...

And to make them even more delicious, add 50g chopped walnuts to the brownie mixture.

Nonno's Welsh Cakes

BISCOTTI GALLESI

Welsh cakes are scone-like biscuits traditionally made with currants or raisins and they can be eaten hot or cold. Romina often made them at university, as her English housemates loved them. They're a real treat with a cup of tea and we like to eat them with a dollop of mascarpone mixed with a little orange zest for an Italian twist.

Makes: 20
Preparation time: 15 minutes
Cooking time: 20–30 minutes

1 large egg, preferably free-range or organic

100g currants, raisins or sultanas

250g self-raising flour

90g caster sugar, plus extra to sprinkle

a pinch of fine salt

30g unsalted butter, at room temperature

90g soft margarine

a splash of milk, if needed

Beat the egg, stir in the currants and set aside while you prepare the dough.

In a large bowl, mix together the flour, sugar and salt. Rub in the butter and margarine. Add the egg-and-raisin mixture and gently combine to form a dough. You may need to add a splash of milk if the mixture is too dry.

On a floured surface, roll out the dough to a thickness of 0.75cm. Using a 5cm round pastry cutter or a glass, cut the dough into circles.

Place a large heavy-bottomed, non-stick frying pan over a low-to-medium heat. (Welsh cakes are traditionally cooked on a cast iron baking stone, but in the absence of one, this should do the trick!) When the pan is hot, place the Welsh cakes in the pan, a few at a time, and cook for about 1½ minutes on each side, until golden brown. If they are turning brown too quickly or burning but not cooking in the middle, lower the heat. If they are taking longer than 2 minutes to cook on each side, turn up the heat, as they will dry out if they are cooked for too long. Transfer the hot Welsh cakes to a plate and sprinkle with a little sugar.

⊗ TIPS

We love to experiment with traditions and sometimes include cinnamon and dried apricots in our Welsh cakes. Just add a teaspoon of ground cinnamon to the flour and replace the currants with the same amount of chopped dried apricots. You could even try white chocolate and dried cranberries . . . the world is your oyster.

It's important to use both butter and margarine in this recipe to get the desired texture in the finished Welsh cakes.

Home from Home

EMILIA ROMAGNA

One of the wealthiest regions of Italy in terms of history, culture and food, Emilia Romagna is full of undiscovered gems. It is the home of Parma ham, Parmesan cheese, mortadella, balsamic vinegar . . . the list goes on. And it has the highest proportion of castles in the world!

Many people will have passed through Emilia Romagna when travelling from Milan to Florence or Rome, but few will have taken the time to explore the region – we recommend you should!

Start with a day and a night in Parma. We would choose this over Florence any time – it is just as impressive but with fewer tourists and amazing food. Walk around the beautiful piazze, visit the cathedral, eat at the I Tre Porcellini (see page 296), and don't forget to try a *gelato* (see page 296). Next, we suggest you drive to Bardi to see the castle. There are not many hotels or other tourist attractions in Bardi (unless you're happy wandering through the mountains and enjoying the landscape and scenery), so visit the castle in the morning and then make your way down to Piacenza or Castell'Arquato. Piacenza is another beautiful city, much like Parma, but Castell'Arquato is a medieval town set on a hill with gorgeous views of the surrounding valleys. There's a great restaurant here called the Ristorante Taverna del Falconiere, found on the Piazza del Municipio.

WHERE TO STAY IN ITALY

. . . ON A BUDGET

Both of these are self-catering apartments, which offer fairly basic amenities but are spotlessly clean and provide all you need if you want to relax and explore the surrounding areas.

Residence Il Borgo, Bellagio

Bellagio is a beautiful town on Lake Como. It's a great base from which to explore the local shops and restaurants and wander down the cobbled streets. You can swim in the lake or hike to nearby *trattorie*. Flavio is the wonderfully friendly owner of a few apartments and he's a brilliant person to know, as he can offer some great local insight. Basic information is on their website, but do give Flavio a call, as he speaks good English and is very helpful.

www.borgoresidence.it/eng

Riomaggiore, Cinque Terre

We are always surprised by how few Brits know about the Cinque Terre. The area is popular with Americans and Australians but we want to see more British tourists in there. The Cinque Terre comprises five cliff towns right on the seafront, set within a National Park (think a northern version of the Amalfi coast). It's a little difficult to get to by car, but the train runs right through each town, so leave your car at La Spezia and hop on! There is also 'La Via dell' Amore' ('The Path of Love'), which connects the five towns. Each town has its own identity but we always stay at Riomaggiore. Edi has some great self-catering apartments and they are always spotlessly clean – ask for a sea view, if possible. And be prepared for lots of hills and steps!

www. appartamenticinqueterre.net

. . . IF YOU'D LIKE TO SPLASH OUT

Sextantio Grotte della Civita, Matera

Matera is one of the most beautiful towns we've ever visited. It is a little like Jerusalem, Petra and a medieval Italian city rolled into one. The town was constructed directly onto the rocks and many homes are actually built into the natural caves. This hotel is run by a group of individuals who restore historical sites to their former glory. They use local suppliers and craftspeople, and any profits are reinvested into similar projects elsewhere. The rooms are within the grottos and caves of an ancient church and they retain their original simplicity – but with the occasional touch of luxury!

www.sextantio.it/grotte-civita

La Bandita, Pienza

This villa is set in the middle of the Tuscan hills. Imagine filmic scenes of rolling olive groves, vineyards, cypress trees and breathtaking countryside. It is an elegant villa with lots of facilities – including a full-time chef, on request. Laid-back luxury, privacy and personal attention are the owners' primary aims. Nearby are Montepulciano and Montalcino, the wine capitals of Tuscany, surrounded by their prized vineyards, Brunello and Vino Nobile. Pienza is a short drive away, famous for its pecorino cheese, and just outside the town is the monastery of Sant'Anna Camprena, which was the location for *The English Patient*. Set in the countryside outside Montalcino, you can still hear Vespers sung in the tenth-century abbey of San Antimo. And Bagno Vignoni is the tiny spa town where travellers have enjoyed hot sulphur springs since Roman times.

www.la-bandita.com

MILAN APERITIVI

We've already discussed Milan's unrivalled aperitivi culture, *and here are our top recommendations. Visit between 6 p.m. and 8 p.m. to enjoy the free buffet with your drink!*

Roialto

Unless you're feeling particularly adventurous, you'll need to get a taxi here, as it's a little way away from the city centre. Try a piña colada cocktail (served in a massive coconut) and enjoy the endless food. If you fancy a boogie afterwards, one of Milan's top nightclubs is just around the corner. Il Gattopardo Café is in a converted church – a bit pretentious and pricey but if you want to check out the city's best-dressed, it's worth a look!

Roialto,
37 Via Giulio Cesare Procaccini, 20154 Milano
www.roialtogroup.it

Il Gattopardo Café,
47 Via Piero della Francesca, 20154 Milano
www.ilgattopardocafe.it

Il Rita

This is a true Milanese spot, free from students and tourists, and well known for its cocktails and *aperitivi*. It is located on the canals (the *navigli*), so you'll need to take the underground to Porta Genova.

1 Via Angelo Fumagalli, 20143 Milano

Exploit

If you're looking for something a little more upmarket, try the rather swanky Exploit, which is a five-minute walk from Piazza del Duomo.

3 Via Pioppette, 20123 Milano
www.exploitmilano.com

Nobu Armani

Whilst this isn't traditional Italian *aperitivi* (Nobu is the internationally acclaimed Japanese chef), if you buy a pricey cocktail you can sample some delicious free sushi that would otherwise cost you a fortune! It is set in the middle of Armani's enormous shopping complex, right in the centre of town.

31 Via Alessandro Manzoni, 20121 Milano
(or 1 Via Pisoni, 20121 Milano)
www.noburestaurants.com/milan

THE BEST TRATTORIE

La Locanda Cacciatore, Piacenza

If you're ever in northern Italy and near Milan or Piacenza, you must try to get to this restaurant. It really is a very special place and fantastic value, too. It serves traditional *trattoria* dishes and is where the locals go for properly cooked Italian food. It is so renowned, the Milanese football team often make the journey just to eat here! We can easily spend four hours eating lunch or dinner. With no written menu, let the waiters choose for you – we recommend their *primi piatti* taster menu so you can sample everything instead of choosing just one dish. If you're lucky, you might get to try their 'roast beef' – but it's nothing like a British Sunday roast! The meat is sliced very thinly and drizzled with lemon juice – it melts in the mouth. You should also try the local red wine, Gutturnio – it's a sparkling red and completely delicious. And don't get us started on the desserts . . .

2 Mistadello Di Castione,
Ponte Dell' Olio, 29028 Piacenza
www.locandacacciatori.com

Il Colombo, Bettola

This pizzeria is in Mum's hometown, Bettola. It is about fifteen minutes' drive into the mountains from Ponte Dell'Olio. We stop here for a pizza before making the final drive up the mountains to our home. A twelve-inch pizza starts from €4 and is one of the best in the region.

2 Piazza Cristoforo Colombo, 29021 Bettola

I Tre Porcellini, Parma

This is another classic Italian restaurant serving fantastic traditional food. Whenever we go to Parma for the day, we make sure we stop here for a lengthy lunch.

60/A Borgo del Correggio, 43121 Parma
www.itreporcellini.biz

THE BEST GELATO

Everyone knows that Italy makes the best ice cream, but you should really go where the locals go to get your scoops.

MILAN

There are two fantastic *gelaterias* in Milan.

Grom

Grom is relatively new. It's actually an Italian chain, which is growing internationally. Located right in the heart of the city centre, it's a stone's throw from the Duomo, and often has queues out the doors. Their philosophy is to use raw, local and seasonal ingredients without additives or colourings.

16 Via Santa Margherita, 20121 Milano
www.grom.it/eng

Gelateria Marghera

This is much further out from the centre – you'll need to take the underground to Wagner. It is very popular with the locals and has a huge variety of flavours.

33 Via Marghera, 20149 Milano

BOLOGNA

La Sorbetteria Castiglione is a ten-minute walk from the city centre. It's a beautiful stroll and you get a real treat at the end.

44 Via Castiglione, 40124 Bologna

PARMA

Nestled right in the centre of Parma, **Gelateria K2** serves their ice cream in a rose pattern – perfect for all you romantics out there! And you can enjoy your ice cream while looking up at the cathedral.

23 Via Fratelli Cairoli, Parma

ROME

Tucked away two streets from the Trevi Fountain is **Il Gelato di San Crispino.**

42 Via della Panetteria, 00187 Roma
www.ilgelatodisancrispino.it

Index

Grazie Mille

At the beginning of 2012, if someone had said to us that we would be writing a cookbook with one of the best publishers in the world and filming a TV series on Channel 4, we would have laughed. But here we are…

Firstly, a HUGE thank you to all at Penguin. It takes great patience to work with one Chiappa girl, but to have to handle all three of us (four, if you include Mum) . . . To Daniel Bunyard, whose introductions kicked all this off – we are eternally grateful. To Lindsey Evans, who saw something in us and decided to go forward with the book (are you crazy?). It has been an incredible experience working with you, and you're now part of the Chiappa family (certainly Mum thinks she's found a NBF!). Hopefully this is the start of a brilliant relationship for many years to come. John Hamilton and Mark Read understood us and took all of our opinions on board. As Dad likes to remind us on a daily basis, your patience will guarantee your 'gateway to heaven'. Sarah Fraser converted the ideas of three demanding ladies on to paper and thanks also to Rahel Weiss for her support. The book looks more incredible than we ever could have imagined. And to everyone else at Penguin including Tom Weldon and Louise Moore, thank you. This book is a dream come true, and it's all because of you.

Thanks to Penguin's belief in us, Fresh One Productions decided to take the plunge and produce *Simply Italian* for Channel 4. THANK YOU to the entire team. If we could write every name on here we would, but you all know who you are! A very special shout-out to Zoe Collins. We are little fish in your massive TV pond and yet you've been unbelievably supportive, putting together a team that blended in perfectly with the madness of the Chiappa family. Thanks to Emma Robertson and Mike Matthews, the visionaries involved in getting the show commissioned in record time, and to Isabel Davis, Ian Carre and Ed St. Giles for making it all happen at a bonkers time of the year for us. *Tantissimi bacini* and *abbracci* to the gorgeous food team, Ginny Rolfe and her *topolini*, and also to Jamie Oliver – we've been amazed and honoured to have had your genuine support from day one. We've had to pinch ourselves so many times working with such experts in the industry! And finally to our wonderful recipe testers, including the La Vieille Ferme team.

Without all the amazing food and recipes Italy has delighted us with over all the summers we've spent there, amongst so many family and friends, we wouldn't be writing this today. Extra special thanks to Paolo Chiappa, our cousin, who put up with us filming and shooting in his bakery and even let us have some of his recipes, and to Case Riglio, Francesca from Il Castello Ricevimenti, chef David Mangan at La Bandita in Tuscany and to all at Il Cacciatore.

Finally, *la famiglia*. Without you, this book wouldn't exist. For some of you, thanks are needed for letting us borrow your recipes, making sure we had the best in the book. For others, including our hugely supportive husbands, the extended Chiappa family and Patching and Starnes in-laws, thank you for your patience and for letting film crews, photographers and generally lots of people descend on your various homes, dinners and family occasions. To our *nonni*, who ingrained Italian traditions in us, we will never forget the memories of endless days making tortelli and ravioli or baking until our hearts were content. To Dad, we love that to this day, you don't understand why people are interested in us; we're just normal girls in your eyes. Thank you for being so patient throughout this entire process. We know your home is your sanctuary, so we're sorry for bringing bucketloads of people to break the silence, but hopefully this book will make up for it. After all, you secretly loved having us home to test all the recipes, didn't you? And to Mum – oh dear, this is where we might get sentimental. You really are the best. Thank you for letting us into the kitchen to learn all your little tips and tricks, for running around after all three of us, and for helping us with everything. You're the master recipe tester, chef and a million other things too. Thank you for always being on the end of the phone whenever we ring you up to ask how to cook something; perhaps this book now means that this can end, as we finally all have our own copy of our family recipes in a book we can cherish for ever.

Grazie mille tutti!

Bacioni,
The Chiappa Sisters,
Michela, Emi and Romina xxx

Buon appetito!